Longman
Preliminary English
Skills

A skills and practice course for the
Cambridge Preliminary English Test

J B HEATON

Longman

Longman Group UK Limited,
Longman House, Burnt Mill, Harlow,
Essex CM20 2JE, England
and Associated Companies throughout the world.

First published 1990
Third impression 1994

Set in linotron 202, 10/12pt Plantin Medium

Produced by Longman Singapore Publishers Pte Ltd
Printed in Singapore

ISBN 0-582-01843-9

CONTENTS

INTRODUCTION

TO THE TEACHER

This book is intended to prepare students for the University of Cambridge **P**reliminary **E**nglish **T**est (PET). Because the Preliminary English Test contains real-life tasks using English, it is possible to use this book both to prepare for the examination and to practise those skills and tasks essential to everyday communication in English.

The activities, exercises and test questions in this book will help students to use English for a wide variety of purposes, all of which are highly relevant in daily life in situations where English is spoken. The material in the book assumes that students have already acquired some formal knowledge of English at a basic level – similar to the situation common in most classrooms throughout the world. In this way, the book seeks to build upon those language skills which students already possess, thereby developing their fluency and confidence in *using* English.

The book closely follows the specifications drawn up for the Preliminary English Test. The following are examples of common situations included in the book: identifying oneself; identifying other people; making and replying to requests, offers, suggestions; giving directions; saying where things are; talking about time; giving information about things; talking about one's likes and dislikes; discussing one's needs; discussing what other people are doing.

Each unit in the book concentrates on the language concerned with a common topic: for example, shopping, houses and flats, health, the weather, transport, schools and colleges, people, holidays, sport, jobs, hobbies, entertainment, countries, food and restaurants.

Although the book contains the types of questions set in the Preliminary English Test, several other useful kinds of questions are also included. The book constantly seeks to provide a wide variety of highly interesting and relevant language tasks and activities.

The units in the book follow the order of the questions in the Preliminary English Test.

TO THE STUDENT

You can use this book with a teacher or on your own. If you use it in class with a teacher, you will be able to take part in pair and group work as well as doing written exercises by yourself both in class and at home. Your teacher will also be able to add other exercises and activities to those provided in this book.

It is also possible to use this book on your own without a teacher. You can find answers to the exercises – and some further notes to help you – in the Teacher's Book. Clearly, if you are working alone, you will not be able to do certain activities (for example, speaking activities where you are asked to work in pairs or groups). However, you will still be able to do most of the exercises and you should find the book helpful for you.

All the following sections will be useful if you are working on your own. The instructions for some of these exercises may say *Work in pairs* or *Work in groups*, but you can still do these exercises if you are working individually.

Practice Test 1: Questions 1–12

Unit 1:   Exercises 1, 2 (part), 3, 4, and 5
Unit 2:   Exercises 1, 2, 3, 4, 5, 6 and 7
Unit 3:   Exercises 2, 3, 4, 5, 6 and 7
Unit 4:   Exercises 1, 2, 3, 4, 5, 6 and 7
Unit 5:   Exercises 1, 3, 5 and 6
Unit 6:   Exercises 2, 3, 4 and 6
Unit 7:   Exercises 1, 3, 4, 6, 7 and 8
Unit 8:   Exercises 2, 3, 4, 5 and 7
Unit 9:   Exercises 1, 2, 3 and 4
Unit 10: Exercises 2, 3, 4, 5, 6 and 7
Unit 11: Exercises 1, 2, 3, 4, 5 and 6
Unit 12: Exercises 1, 2, 5, 6, 7 and 8
Unit 13: Exercises 1, 3, 4 and 7
Unit 14: Exercises 1, 3, 4, 5, 6 and 7
Unit 15: Exercises 2, 3, 4, 5, 6 and 7
Unit 16: Exercises 1, 3, 4, 5, 6, 7 and 8

Practice Test 2: Questions 1–12

Students working on their own are strongly advised to study the section on Techniques on page 112.

PRACTICE TEST 1

OVERVIEW

Preparing for the Preliminary English Test (PET) and learning to *use* English involve the same skills. The Preliminary English Test is a communicative type of test which uses everyday situations and activities as language tasks. All the exercises, activities and test items in this book have been written to make active and develop those language skills which are necessary not only for the test itself but also for real life.

The Preliminary English Test consists of 4 parts: reading, writing, listening and speaking. The reading and writing parts of the test take 1½ hours, the listening part takes approximately 20 minutes, and the speaking part almost 10 minutes.

Reading

Question 1	Short text: public notices, signs, etc (Photographs, drawings)	Multiple-choice items
Question 2	Text: usually an event, a story, etc (Blanks in text)	Texts with blanks to be filled by multiple-choice items
Question 3	Short text containing essential information only (sometimes with drawings and diagrams)	Usually matching items, box-ticking items and multiple-choice items (but not of ordinary kind)
Question 4	Text: advertisements, public notices, brochures	Usually true/false items, box-ticking items (and NOT multiple-choice)
Question 5	Text for general comprehension, deduction of its likely source and intended audience	Multiple-choice, short-answer questions

Writing

Question 6	Structural exercise (usually five sentences on same theme)	Transformation of sentences (ie rewriting sentences in different way)
Question 7	Directed writing (about 75 words)	Form-filling, note-making, messages
Question 8	Free writing (often about recent events, future plans, etc)	Letter, etc based on diary or in answer to another letter, advertisement, etc

Listening

Question 9	Short statements and conversations (one speaker and two speakers)	Multiple-choice items in form of diagrams, drawings, photographs, etc
Question 10	Talk, report, etc giving information about travel, weather, opening times, etc	Mostly box-ticking questions
Question 11	Radio programmes, etc: news, reports about recent events, general interest reports	Questions requiring short written answers, writing numbers, etc
Question 12	Discussion between two or three people: holiday plans, remembering something which has happened, etc	Mostly true/false items testing ability to recognise general meaning, agreement, disagreement, apologies, complaints, etc

Speaking

Section 1	Talking about oneself, giving information about things	General conversation about home, studies, family, etc. Also spelling name, address, etc and reading out a (phone) number
Section 2	Giving directions, talking about time, discussing needs, making and replying to requests, offers, suggestions	Role-playing using card giving situation and tasks to be performed
Section 3	Describing other people, discussing what others are doing, saying where things are	Talking about a photograph, picture, brochure, etc
Section 4	Discussing likes and dislikes	General conversation starting from picture in Section 3

Now try to do the following test. First do the **Reading and Writing** parts of the test on your own. Complete this part of the test in EXACTLY 1½ hours. Work through the paper quickly but carefully. Look through each question before you begin to answer it. Try to answer every part of the question and do not leave any blanks. If you cannot give an answer, think carefully about the question and then make a careful guess. Remember that you cannot score any marks for a blank.

Next listen to the tape recording of the **Listening** part of the test. Look at the appropriate page in the test as you listen and then answer the question according to the instructions on the tape and in your book.

Finally, do the **Speaking** part of the test IN PAIRS. First one student should pretend to be the examiner and ask the questions in the test, and the other student should be the candidate. Then the students should change parts, and the student who was the examiner should now be the candidate.

READING

Question 1 Look at the following five pictures of signs.
Someone asks you what each sign means. For each sign put a tick in one of the boxes – like this ✓ –
to show the correct answer.

1.

OPEN
Mon – Fri
7.00am to 7.00pm

☐ This shop is open after seven o'clock in the evening from Mondays to Fridays.

☐ You can buy things from the shop only on Mondays and Fridays.

☐ This shop is open for twelve hours each day except on Saturdays and Sundays.

☐ You can't buy things from the shop at lunchtime.

2.

ODEON 1
Separate performances
Cartoons: 2.25 4.30 6.35
Superman: 2.50 4.55 7.00
Ends 8.30

☐ You will miss ten minutes of the main film if you go in the cinema at 3 pm.

☐ The last showing of *Superman* is at half-past eight.

☐ In each performance the cartoons last for over an hour.

☐ There are six different films showing at this cinema.

3.

BREAKFAST
now being served

LUNCH   12 – 2
DINNER   7 – 9

☐ You can have lunch or dinner now.

☐ Breakfast is served from midday until two o'clock.

☐ You can have breakfast now.

☐ Dinner is served after nine in the evening.

4.

**Press button
and wait
until green light shows
before you cross**

☐ Wait until it is safe before you show your anger.

☐ The machine will not start until the green light shows.

☐ A green light will shine in front of you until you press the button.

☐ Press the button but don't walk across the road until the green light shows.

5.

Private property

KEEP OUT

☐ Don't open this letter as it is private.

☐ You cannot enter because this place belongs to someone.

☐ You must not touch this object because it belongs to someone.

☐ This building has been kept open for public use.

Question 2 Read the article below and circle the letter next to the word that best fits each space.

Example: Have you ever .... Portugal?

A. been   (B.) visited   C. gone   D. stayed

The Algarve, Portugal's beautiful sunny (1) ...., is an interesting mixture of (2) .... old villages and modern (3) .... centres with lots of large international hotels. The Atlantic shore is lined with tall cliffs and long sandy (4) .... Small fishing villages are clustered round tiny picturesque (5) .... full of small colourful boats. (6) .... the pace of life is still (7) .... and unhurried, the Algarve offers plenty of activities for today's holidaymakers – (8) .... ranging from golf and tennis to sea-fishing (9) .... plenty of first-class restaurants and nightclubs. Shopping is a very popular pastime with most tourists (10) .... everywhere there are shops full of attractive local crafts at bargain prices.

---

(1)	A beach	B sea	C scene	D coast
(2)	A asleep	B sleepy	C sleeping	D slept
(3)	A tourist	B visitor	C holidaymaker	D traveller
(4)	A coasts	B shores	C beaches	D lands
(5)	A ports	B landings	C harbours	D docks
(6)	A After	B Since	C When	D Although
(7)	A leisurely	B slowly	C quietly	D gently
(8)	A exercises	B sports	C games	D matches
(9)	A but also	B instead of	C rather than	D as well as
(10)	A therefore	B as	C but	D if

Question 3

A   THE FOX INN

16th century village inn situated at the foot of beautiful Mount Kellett. Hot pies, roast beef and Yorkshire pudding, steak. **E, NC, L, P**

B   COCINA

Hot, spicy Mexican food. Good service, candle-lit tables, cosy atmosphere. Specialities: chilli con carne, baked banana dessert, tropical mango cocktail. **B, L**

C   MR NATURAL

For fresh, natural and tasty vegetarian dishes. Italian specialities: Garlic mushrooms, pasta Milanese, aubergine Parmagiana. **D, NS, P**

D   SANG SANG

Traditional Chinese dishes. Specialities: Peking duck, sweet and sour pork. Special arrangements for parties of 12 or more. **C, L, P**

E   THE BASTILLE

Experience an evening with a difference. Wait behind bars in the cells of this imitation of the notorious French prison. Be served by a friendly gaoler. Excellent French wine and genuine French food. **A, L**

F   MACDONELL'S

Tasty beefburgers and fishburgers for all the family. 18 different kinds of ice-cream. Puzzles and painting books given to all children under 12. Self-service. **E, P, NS.**

KEY

Price per person for a 3-course/complete meal

A: Over £20;   B: £16–£20;   C: £11–£15;   D: £6–£10;   E: Under £6.

NC: No children   *L: Alcoholic drinks available*
NS: No smoking areas   *P: Parking*

Read the information about restaurants in Harehills. The following people are looking for somewhere to have a meal. Read the sentences below and decide which of the six restaurants is the most suitable for each person or couple.

1. Mr and Mrs Lindstrom don't eat meat and prefer healthy food.
2. Mrs Izumi doesn't like European food and also cannot stand any dishes which are very spicy.
3. Mr and Mrs Rozario want to take their four young children out to a meal on their eldest child's tenth birthday.
4. Mr and Mrs Manton want to go to a restaurant in their small car. Both are quite old and cannot walk far. They want a hot meal under £10 each but they prefer English food, expecially meat dishes. Mr Manton sometimes likes a glass of beer with his meal.
5. Graham and Eva Low want to take about 20 guests out for a meal. Although they like hot and spicy food, they think that some of their guests might not. However, they want something different from the English food which they eat every day.
6. Mr Al-Omani is taking a business friend out for a meal. He doesn't mind how much he spends on the meal but he wants it to be very good and, if possible, a little different from most other restaurants so that his guest will remember it.
7. Francisco Martinez wants to take his wife out for a meal on her birthday. They both like hot food with plenty of spices. He can't afford to spend more than £40 on a meal for both of them.
8. Linda Short and Maria Baptista don't enjoy eating at all if anyone near them is smoking. They don't mind what food they eat but they want to be served at their table by waiters or waitresses.

Fill in the letter A, B, C, D, E or F to show which restaurant you think is the most suitable.

Mr and Mrs Lindstrom ....
Mrs Izumi ....
Mr and Mrs Rozario ....
Mr and Mrs Manton ....
Graham and Eva Low ....
Mr Al-Omani ....
Francisco Martinez ....
Linda Short and Maria Baptista ....

Question 4

BEIJING	HONG KONG	SEOUL	SINGAPORE	TOKYO
Mostly sunny somewhat cool, high 56, low 38. **Friday:** sunny, milder, high 59, low 36.	Cloudy rain or drizzle, high 69, low 56. **Friday:** cool, high 65, low 53.	High clouds clearing later, high 52, low 39. **Friday:** sunny, high 56, low 36.	Hazy, humid thunder nearby, high 89, low 78. **Friday:** thunderstorms, high 90, low 77.	Sunny early rain later, high 58, low 47. **Friday:** rain ending, high 62, low 43.

World Weather

You are on a tour of East Asia and you want to check the weather report in an American newspaper. Remember that today is Thursday. If you think a statement below is correct, put a tick (√) in the box. If you think it is incorrect, put a cross (×) in the box.

1. It will be a little warmer tomorrow in Beijing than it is today. ☐

2. It may rain later today in Seoul. ☐

3. There will be a lot of showers in Tokyo tomorrow evening. ☐

4. The weather in Tokyo will become worse later today. ☐

5. The weather in Singapore will improve tomorrow. ☐

6. Canton will be as cool as Shanghai today. ☐

7. Temperatures in Kuala Lumpur and Singapore will be about the same. ☐

8. It will be slightly hotter in Kuala Lumpur than in Bangkok today. ☐

9. The temperatures in Hong Kong will fall a little by tomorrow. ☐

10. The temperature will be over 100°F in Dacca today. ☐

Question 5 Read this passage and then answer the questions which follow. You must tick the correct box or write in a few words.

Channel 4: 2.30 – 4.15

MIRACLE IN MILAN
1951 (Black and White)

Vittorio De Sica, the director of *Miracle in Milan*, followed his extraordinarily successful *Bicycle Thieves* with another story about the poor people of Italy. While *Bicycle Thieves* is a realistic drama, true to life in every detail, *Miracle in Milan* is like a charming fairy story. In spite of its lack of realism, however, *Miracle in Milan* is both an excellent commentary on Italian society and a very moving film about real people and the problems of Italian society at the time.

The story is about a small boy, Toto, who grows up to do only good. The boy helps the poor of Milan to build a village of old huts in the suburbs of the city. When oil is discovered on the site of the village, however, the wealthy owner of the land tries to send the poor peasants away.

A few hard-headed viewers may find parts of the film artificial and unnatural. Indeed, this heart-warming film could so easily have gone completely wrong, but in the sensitive hands of De Sica, a small masterpiece emerges – even though the leading roles were played by non-professional actors. Most viewers will undoubtedly be touched by the film's simplicity and innocence. This is definitely a film not to be missed.

1. This piece of writing is from

   ☐ a film script.

   ☐ an advertisement.

   ☐ a TV programme guide.

   ☐ a news story.

2. What is the film *Miracle in Milan* trying to do?

   ☐ Present simply a charming fairy story.

   ☐ Show how non-professional actors can help to make a small masterpiece.

   ☐ Make people sad through its simple and innocent story.

   ☐ Express a view of Italian society by means of a simple but moving story.

3. What do you think Toto does after the discovery of the village?

   ....

4. Vittorio De Sica's previous film was different from *Miracle in Milan* because ....

   ....

5. The writer of the passage

   ☐ highly recommends the film.

   ☐ recommends the film to a certain degree.

   ☐ does not really recommend the film at all.

   ☐ neither recommends the film nor criticises it.

WRITING

Question 6 Here are some sentences about houses and flats. Finish the second sentence so that it has the same meaning as the first.

Example: Each of the new flats has four large rooms and a modern kitchen.

There *are four large rooms and a modern kitchen in each of the new flats*.

1. It isn't necessary to pay in full for a flat at once.

   You ....

2. Certain banks will lend you the money to buy one.

   You can ....

3. The flats on the top floor are more expensive than those on the first floor.

   The flats on the first floor ....

4. They can paint each room in any colour you want.

   Each room ....

5. Most of the flats have already been sold even though the prices are very high.

   Most of the flats have already been sold in spite of ....

Question 7 You have gone to a new doctor. He has asked you to complete a health form giving details about yourself.

Surname ....(Mr/Mrs/Miss/Ms) *Circle correct title*

Other names ....

Date of birth .... Place of birth ....

Home address ....

....

....

....

Occupation ....

Name of company/school/college ....

Number of days this year you have been absent through illness ....

Name of illness(es) ....

Have you ever been in hospital? YES/NO *Circle the correct answer*

If YES, please give dates and details ....

....

What is your weight? .... How tall are you? ....

Favourite dish/food ....

Type of food eaten most often ....

Do you do exercise or play games regularly? YES/NO *Circle the correct answer*

If YES, give details and state how often ....

....

....

Please give any other details about your health and physical fitness.

....

....

Signature .... Date ....

Question 8 Imagine that this is your diary showing your activities on certain days. First, fill in your activities for those days which have been left blank. Then use the information in your diary to write a letter to a friend. Tell him or her how you are spending your time. Write about 100 words. The address is not necessary.

1	MONDAY	Started school!
2	TUESDAY	Table-tennis. Cinema
3	WEDNESDAY	Chosen for school hockey team
4	THURSDAY	
5	FRIDAY	Joined School Photography Club.
6	SATURDAY	Shopping, then cycling
7	SUNDAY	

....

....

....

....

....

....

....

....

LISTENING

Question 9 Listen to the conversations on the tape. Put a tick in the box you think is the most suitable.

1.

2.

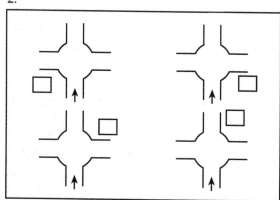

3.

4.

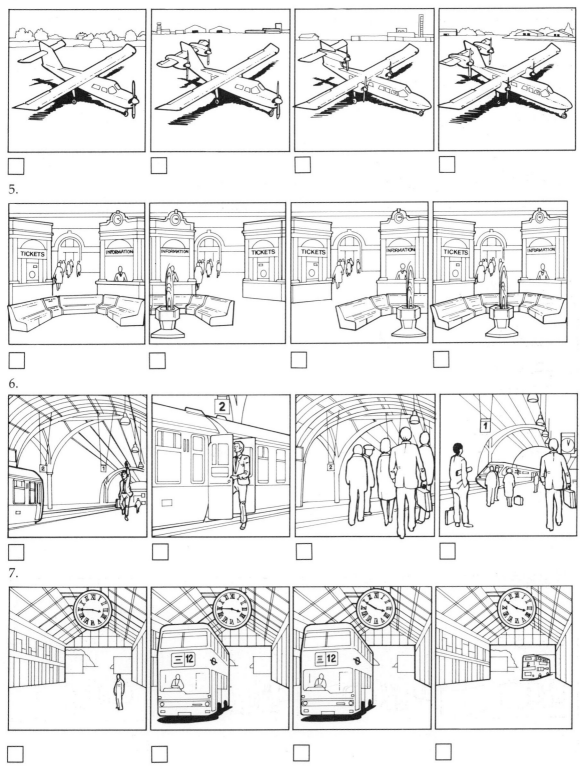

5.

6.

7.

Question 10 Listen to these sports results. In the notes below put a tick in the boxes after the names of the winners.

1	*Basketball*		*4*	*Athletics*	
	Burnley	☐		France	☐
	Netton	☐		England	☐
	Gargrave	☐		Spain	☐
	Settle	☐		Italy	☐
2	*Table Tennis*		*5*	*Swimming*	
	Thorpe	☐		Linda Thomas	☐
	Linton	☐		Eva Chan	☐
	Burnsall	☐		Tina Hall	☐
	Bolton	☐		Maggie Low	☐
3	*Badminton*		*6*	*Motor Racing*	
	Oakworth	☐		Ricki Alberti	☐
	Stanhope	☐		Dan Pirelli	☐
	Bramley	☐		Hal Stewart	☐
	Clifton	☐		Nelson Mantillet	☐

Question 11 Write in the information needed below and put a tick in the boxes you think are the most suitable.

THE LAND OF THE SHERPAS

There are several different tribes:

eg Sherpas (famous as ....)

Gurkhas (famous as ....)

Kanchenjunga is in the:

north of Nepal ☐   east of Nepal ☐   west of Nepal ☐   south of Nepal ☐

The southern part of Nepal contains .... and ....

Sal is used for ....

The following animals live in the jungles of Nepal:

lions ☐   tigers ☐   wolves ☐   leopards ☐

elephants ☐   bears ☐   giraffes ☐   rhinoceros ☐

The main exports are: rice ☐   wheat ☐   jute ☐   sugar ☐

The population of Nepal is ....

Question 12 if you agree with the statement, put a tick in the box under 'Yes'. If you do not agree, put a tick in the box under 'No'.

	YES	NO
1. The man usually likes going shopping with his wife.	☐	☐
2. He doesn't really want to buy a new video recorder, but they need one.	☐	☐
3. The man has just bought a new camera.	☐	☐
4. The man often likes to buy toys for their children.	☐	☐
5. The woman is very careful and always wants to save money.	☐	☐

SPEAKING: A

Section I

Answer the questions which your partner (or your teacher) asks you about yourself.

PARTNER/TEACHER: Ask the following questions (or similar questions):

What's your name?

Where are you from?

What's the name of the street where you live?

Can you spell it?

How did you get here today?

Why are you learning English?

Section II

You are in a shop which sells cameras and films. You want to buy a camera like the one in the picture on page 117 but you cannot pay more than £50 for one. You can pay cash as you've brought the money with you.

Your partner (or your teacher) is the shop assistant. Talk about what you want: the kind of camera, the price, what you decide. First, look at the picture on page 117.

PARTNER/TEACHER: Say that you are the shop assistant. Then say:

Good morning. Can I help you?

....

We have two main types of cameras: automatic and manual. Automatic cameras do everything for you: just point the camera and take the picture. If you use a manual camera, you must set the camera according to the amount of light and the distance.

....

Do you want a camera with a flash so that you can take pictures indoors?

....

Do you want a fairly cheap camera or an expensive one?

....

This red camera here costs £48 and the black one over there costs £64.

....

Do you want to pay by credit card, cheque or cash?

....

Thank you very much. I'm sure you'll be very happy with this camera.

Section III

Look at the photograph on the first page of the colour section in the centre of the book and tell your partner or your teacher about it.

TALK ABOUT:
  what the people are doing
  what kind of clothes they are wearing
  how they probably feel
  in what ways they are similar
  in what ways they are different
  where they are

Section IV

Now talk to your partner or your teacher and try to answer the questions which are asked.

PARTNER/TEACHER: Ask the following questions or similar questions of your own:

Do you like playing table tennis?

....

(If yes)   How often do you play?
(If no)   What sports or games do you like?

....

(Say something about the sports and games you yourself like or dislike. Then ask another question.)
What do you enjoy most about ---?

....

Is there anything you don't like about ---?

....

Why do you think it's good to play games or have a hobby?

....

(Give your opinion and then ask other questions or finish the conversation.)

SPEAKING: B

Section I

Answer the questions which your partner (or your teacher) asks you about yourself.

PARTNER/TEACHER: Ask the following questions (or similar questions):

What's your name?
Is that your full name?
Can you spell your surname?
Where have you lived most of your life?
What's your address?
What's your phone number or the number of a telephone which can be used to reach you?
What do you find difficult about learning English?

Section II

Your cassette recorder has broken. It will play tapes but it won't record. You take it to the shop where you bought it about two years ago. You want your cassette recorder repaired.
Your partner (or your teacher) is the shop assistant. Talk about the cassette recorder, the problem, when it will be ready, the cost, and what you decide. First, look at the picture on page 117.

PARTNER/TEACHER: Say that you are the shop assistant. Then say:

Good morning. Can I help you?

....

What exactly is the problem?

....

Did you buy the cassette recorder from us?

....

How long have you had it?

....

Is there anything else wrong with it?

....

Well, I think we'll be able to repair it without too much difficulty.

....

It'll probably be about two weeks before it's ready.

....

I can't say for certain until we've examined it. I should think it'll cost about £20.

Section III

Look at Picture A on the second page of the colour section in the centre of the book and tell your partner or your teacher about it.

TALK ABOUT:
   the type of house
   the garage
   the garden
   what the person is doing in the garden

Now look at Picture B on the second page of the colour section and tell your partner or your teacher what differences you can see.

TALK ABOUT:
   the house and garden
   what the people are doing
   what kind of people you think they are

Section IV

Now talk to your partner or your teacher and try to answer the questions which are asked.

PARTNER/TEACHER: Say that the two pictures are from a news magazine. Ask the following questions or similar questions of your own.

Do you like reading newspapers and magazines?

....

(If yes)   How often do you read them?
(If no)   What do you like reading?

....

(Say something about the magazines or books you yourself like or dislike. Then ask another question.)
What kind of stories do you enjoy most?

....

Do you read anything in English? If so, what?

....

Why do you think it's good to read a lot?

....

What are your hobbies or favourite pastimes?

....

(Now ask other questions or finish the conversation.)

About Yourself

1 Listen to the two short conversations on tape. Write down information about the two people being interviewed under the following headings:

NAME
HOME TOWN OR CITY
DISTRICT OR VILLAGE
MEANS OF TRAVEL

2 Work in small groups. Look at Mandy's family tree.

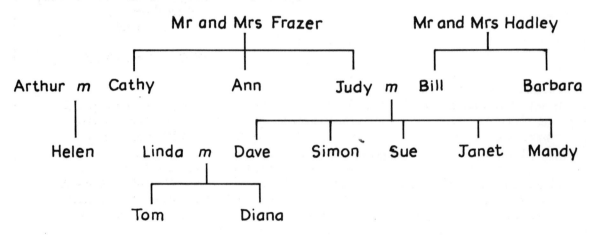

1 What are Mandy's grandparents called?
2 How many aunts has Mandy got?
3 How many brothers and sisters has she got?
4 Can you see any only children in this family tree?
   (Note: An only child is someone without brothers or sisters.)
5 What are the names of Mandy's nephew and niece?
6 How many grandchildren have Mr and Mrs Frazer got?

Now draw your own family tree. Then work in small groups. Ask the others in the group about their families and answer questions about your own family.

3 Some puzzles. Listen to each short conversation on tape. Can you guess what relation each person is to the speaker? Write down your answers in your exercise books.

EXAMPLE:
A: Who's Maria? I don't think I've met her.
B: Surely you've met Maria. She's my father's daughter. Do you know who she is now?

ANSWER:
Maria is your *sister* .

1 Fernando is your _____ .
2 Juanita and Alberto are your _____ .
3 Mr and Mrs Branco are your _____ .
4 Pedro is your _____ .
5 He is your _____ .

4 Read the following letter from a student in Thailand to a penfriend in Britain. Then use the information to complete the form below.

> 267, Sukhumvit Lane 13,
> Bangkok 11,
> Thailand.
>
> 25 October, 1989.
>
> Dear Sharon,
>   My name is Wipa Siraporn and I am in the 4th grade at Petburi College. I am very happy to be your penfriend because I want to learn about England. I like learning English and I want to improve as much as I can.
>   I am fifteen years old, and my birthday was on September 30th. My father is a clerk in a small import and export company in Bangkok and my mother works in a small clothing factory near our house. I have three sisters and two brothers, and they are all students, too.
>   I haven't lived in Bangkok all my life. I was born in Chengmai and I lived there until I was eight.
>   I like pop music and collecting postcards from foreign countries. I also like swimming. What do you like doing?
>   I'm looking forward to hearing from you soon. Goodbye for now.
>
>   Yours truly,
>   Wipa

Surname:	Other name(s):
Date of birth:	Place of birth:
School/College:	
Home address:	
Hobbies/Sports:	

5 Now write a short letter about yourself to an English penfriend called Stephen. Use the model below and write your letter out in full. You can make up the details if you prefer.

> (your address)
> (today's date)
>
> Dear Stephen
>   My name is _____ (your name) and I am in _____ (your class) at _____ (your school/college). I would be very happy to be your penfriend because _____ (your reason).
>   I am _____ years old (your age). My father is a _____ (your father's job) in _____ (where your father works) and my mother _____ (what your mother does). I have _____ sisters and _____ brothers (the number of sisters and brothers you have. If you do not have any, write I am an only child).
>   I like _____ and _____ (your hobbies or sports). What do you like doing?
>   I'm looking forward to hearing from you soon. Goodbye for now.
>   Yours truly
>
> _____ (your first name)

6 Work in pairs. Take it in turns to ask and answer the following questions.

1 What's your name?
2 What's your home town?
3 What's the name of your street?
4 Can you spell that, please?
5 I don't know where that is. Could you tell me?
6 Could you tell me the number of your house or flat?
7 How did you get here today?
8 Why are you learning English?
9 Do you have any brothers or sisters?
10 Are they learning English, too?

Signs

1 There are ten hidden words in the word square. The words are all in a straight line: some can be read forwards from left to right and others can be read downwards from top to bottom. You must never miss or jump letters. All the words in the puzzle are taken from shop signs, road signs, etc. The definitions of these words are given under the puzzle to help you.

d	g	a	h	i	r	e	b	k	o	w
t	o	s	w	e	s	s	a	l	p	a
r	p	a	r	k	i	n	g	o	r	r
a	h	l	x	o	b	u	p	c	o	n
l	t	e	r	m	i	n	u	s	p	i
l	f	d	e	c	h	a	r	g	e	n
o	l	a	p	o	e	v	c	u	r	g
w	g	a	n	o	l	o	h	t	t	s
e	i	m	s	e	c	o	a	z	y	b
d	u	s	t	a	l	l	s	e	l	m
v	w	u	b	a	k	l	e	s	x	r

1 pay money to use something for a certain length of time
2 a certain length of time when goods in a shop are sold at lower prices than usual
3 station at the end of a railway line or stop at the end of a bus route
4 possessions, something you own
5 seats on the ground floor of a cinema or theatre
6 leaving your car in a particular place for a time
7 price asked for something
8 buy
9 telling someone about something which may be dangerous or bad
10 let, permitted

2   Can you guess the meaning of each of the words in bold type? Each word appears in a notice. Try to find out its meaning from the rest of the sentence. Write out the letter (A, B, C or D) of the correct answer.

1

Bicycles for
HIRE
£1.00 a day

A   sale at a very low price
B   exchange for new ones
C   loan or use for a time
D   repair and painting

2

A   increased in price   C   made better in quality
B   unchanged in quality   D   made lower in price

3

STUDENT
wants to **rent**
small flat
near Shepley College
for one year

A   pay money regularly to live in
B   clean and paint for a small charge
C   sell for a low price
D   take care of for a small payment

4

SALE now on.
Plenty of
bargains.

A   high quality goods
B   goods sold cheaply
C   useful goods
D   second-hand or used goods

5

Road narrows
No **overtaking**
Single lane only

A   stopping
B   passing
C   parking
D   waiting

3   What words are missing in the following notices? Put in the missing words and rewrite each notice, making it into a complete sentence.

EXAMPLE:
   President Gancia now in London on short visit
   President Gancia is now in London on a short visit.

1   Timson's summer sale starts Monday
2   Buses for London depart Victoria Street Bus Station
3   Fasten seat belts
4   Meals now being served
5   Train from Southampton arrives 7.30
6   Press button and wait
7   Wait until green light appears
8   Hot food available on request

4 Work in pairs. Where would you see the following signs?

Open 9 am – 7 pm Delicious cakes Fresh bread from 11am	Shampoo £2.00 Cutting £3.50 _____ All styles available	10.45 to London now departs from Platform 3	**FEEDING TIMES** 11 am and 5 pm
1	2	3	4

4-star petrol £1.90 Oil and tyres checked while you wait	NOW SHOWING *The Spy Returns* 2.30, 5.20, 8.30	Routes 1, 4, 23 and 27 QUEUE THIS SIDE	*Now being served* BUSINESS LUNCH only £3.20
5	6	7	8

5 Here are some announcements. Listen to each announcement on the tape. Then write out the letter of the picture which you think is most suitable.

1

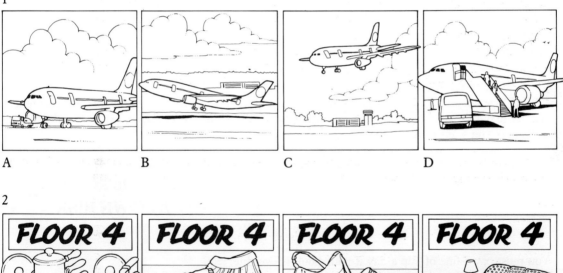

A   B   C   D

2

A   B   C   D

3

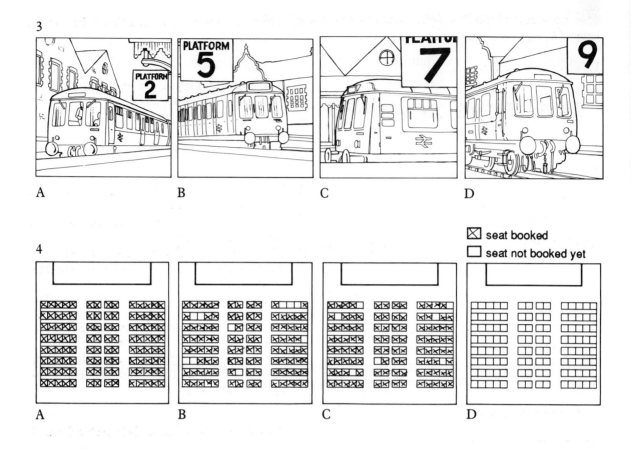

A   B   C   D

4

☒ seat booked
☐ seat not booked yet

A   B   C   D

6   Work in small groups. Each group should design and write a sign for each of the following sentences. Remember to put the sentences in note form. Miss out words like *is, are, a, the, at, one*, etc, and make any other changes you want in word order, etc.

EXAMPLE:

You can leave your coat here but it is at your own risk.

> **All coats left here**
> **AT OWN RISK**

1   You must pay a fine of 10p a day if your book is overdue.
2   You cannot bring back any goods after you have bought them and taken them out of the shop.
3   If you touch any of the goods and accidentally break any of them, you will have to pay the full amount for them.
4   The library is open from ten o'clock to seven o'clock on Mondays, Wednesdays, Thursdays, Fridays and Saturdays but it is open only from ten o'clock to one o'clock on Tuesdays.
5   Children who are under the age of fifteen and adults who are over sixty years of age can travel for half the ordinary fare.

7 Look at the following signs. Someone asks you what each sign means. For each sign write out the letters (A, B, C or D) of the correct answer.

1 SHOPS AND SERVICES

SALE STARTS ON MONDAY

A You must pay for goods before Monday.
B The shop is closed on Monday.
C Prices of goods will be lower on Monday.
D The shop will be sold on Monday.

2 CINEMAS AND THEATRES

Tonight's performance	Stalls £6.50
	Circle £4.50
	Upper Circle £3.00 *(fully booked)*

A The cheapest seats available for tonight are in the upper circle.
B It costs £2.00 more for a seat in the circle than one in the upper circle.
C The most expensive seats are in the circle.
D There are no seats under £4.50 for tonight's performance.

3 RESTAURANTS

Tea, coffee, cola, fruit juices, sandwiches and cakes served all day.

Steak and kidney pie, fish and chips, pizzas
11 – 2. 5 – 7.

A Hot food is not served between 2 and 5 pm.
B You cannot get any cold drinks here.
C You must take sandwiches and cakes away to eat.
D Snacks such as sandwiches are not served between 5 and 7 pm.

4 TRAVEL INFORMATION

SEAT BELTS   NO SMOKING

A Passengers should fasten their seat belts and stop smoking.
B You must not fasten your seat belt if you are smoking.
C You must not smoke unless your seat belt is fastened.
D There are seat belts on the plane but there aren't any cigarettes.

5 ROAD SIGNS

NO PARKING
8.30 a.m - 6.00 p.m
Mon - Sat

A You can't park here at any time from Monday to Saturday.
B You can park here after six o'clock in the evening.
C You can park here from half-past eight to six o'clock each day.
D You can't park here all day Sunday but you can park on Saturday.

6 MISCELLANEOUS WARNINGS

BREAK GLASS
IN CASE OF FIRE

A The glass cannot be broken when there is a fire.
B The glass has been broken in a fire.
C The glass is in a case which may catch fire.
D The glass should be broken if there is a fire.

UNIT THREE

Shopping

1 Work in pairs.

STUDENT A:
Look at the three sets of pictures below. Choose one picture in the first set and describe it to Student B.

STUDENT B:
Listen to Student A's short description and guess which of the pictures was described.

STUDENT B:
Describe one of the second set of pictures.

STUDENT A:
Now listen to Student B's description and guess which picture was described.

1

 A
 B
 C

2

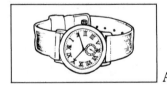 A
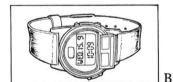 B
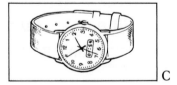 C

2 Here is a conversation between a girl and a shop assistant. Write out the conversation, completing each blank with the missing word. Choose the word from the following list.

cost	charge	bargain	pay	price	buy

CINDY: I'd like to (1) _____ a camera, please.

SHOP ASSISTANT: How much do you want to (2) _____ for one?

CINDY: About £50.

SHOP ASSISTANT: This one on the top shelf is very good. It used to (3) _____ £80 but the (4) _____ has recently been reduced and now it's only £54. It's a real (5) _____ .

CINDY: Do you have a case for it?

SHOP ASSISTANT: Yes, we have. Normally they're £12 but you can have one free of (6) _____ with this particular camera.

3 Copy the following plan of Taski's Department Store into your exercise book. Then listen to the short conversation on tape. As you listen, write the names of the missing departments in the blank spaces on the plan.

Stationery and Books	. . . .	. . . .
. . . .		Sports Goods
Women's Clothes		. . . .
. . . .		Ladies' Jewellery

Main entrance

4 Look again at the plan of Taski's Department Store. Write the name of the department where you must go to buy each of the following goods:

a hockey stick   a dress   a ballpoint pen
a saucepan   a ring   a shirt

5 Look at the five notices below. Someone asks you what each notice means. For each notice write out the letter (A, B, C or D) of the correct answer.

1

Closed for lunch   1 pm–2pm daily

A   This hotel serves lunch for one hour every day.
B   This office does not open in the afternoons.
C   This restaurant serves lunch every day before 1 pm.
D   This shop will not open at lunchtime between 1 and 2.

2

SALE Last day!

A   This shop will not be open today.
B   Goods will be sold at lower prices for a few days only.
C   Goods will be sold at normal prices again tomorrow.
D   This shop will close tomorrow.

3

CIGARETTES not sold to anyone under 18

A   You have to be 18 before you can buy cigarettes.
B   You cannot buy cigarettes if you are only 18.
C   You can buy packets containing fewer than 18 cigarettes.
D   You cannot buy under 18 cigarettes in a packet.

4

TANDIO

portable radios
temporarily out of stock

A   Tandio portable radios have been sold out but more will be on sale at a later date.
B   Tandio portable radios are no longer being made and no more will be sold.
C   Tandio portable radios will soon be all sold as a lot of people are buying them.
D   Tandio portable radios should be bought now because no more will be made.

5

FOR SALE
•   **all makes of watches**   •
from £200 to £2!

A   Both cheap and expensive watches are made here.
B   The watches sold here have all been made by the same firm.
C   Some £200 watches have been reduced to £2.
D   You can get a watch here for as little as £2 or as much as £200.

6 Read the following short statements. Each statement goes with four pictures. Look at each set of pictures and then write the letter of the picture to which the particular statement is referring.

1

Mrs Swallow doesn't sell books any more. Her shop is now a stationer's and you can buy lots of paper and pens there. She also sells magazines.

2

I wonder where I can buy some medicine to make my throat better. I don't want to go to the doctor's and I've heard that Taunus Linctus is very good indeed for sore throats.

3

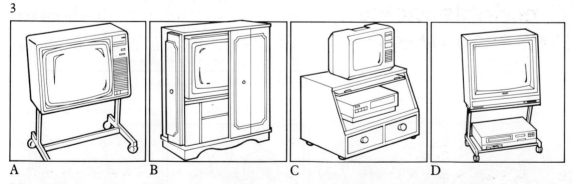

I bought a new colour television set and a video recorder yesterday. I also managed to get a special stand free of charge. The stand has a small shelf on which you can put the video recorder.

7 Listen to the conversations on the tape. Write out the letter (A, B, C or D) of the most suitable picture.

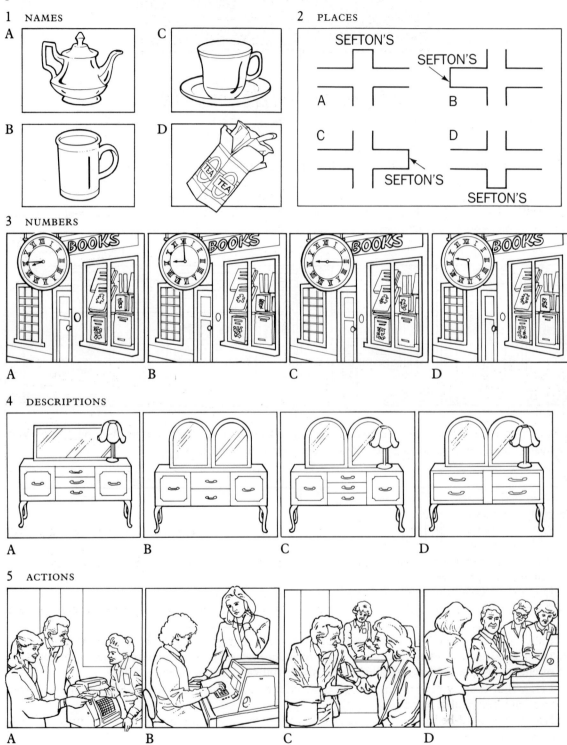

1 NAMES

A

C

B

D

2 PLACES

3 NUMBERS

A   B   C   D

4 DESCRIPTIONS

A   B   C   D

5 ACTIONS

A   B   C   D

Houses and Flats

1 Look at the pictures below and match them with the advertisements which follow.

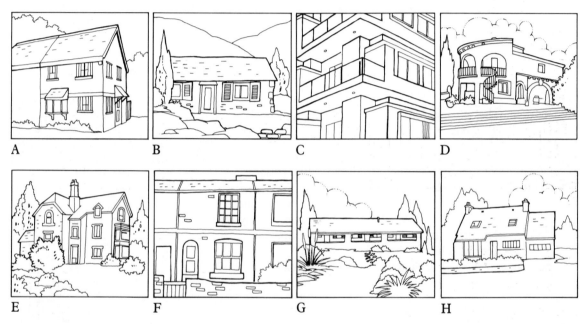

Property for sale in Europe

1 A very attractive small detached house situated in a quiet area near Paris. One lounge, large hall, modern kitchen, three bedrooms.
2 Why not buy your own villa in Spain? Six beautiful villas are now being offered for sale, each over-looking a quiet beach.
3 Charming old cottage for sale in quiet Italian village.
4 A most comfortable semi-detached house situated on the outskirts of Antwerp. Close to shops, schools and station.
5 Fully furnished modern bungalow (4 bedrooms) with large garden in high-class area in Rome.
6 Luxury flat on 2nd floor of modern block of flats close to centre of Lisbon. Lift, security guards, large reception area, swimming pool and tennis courts.
7 Large 19th-century mansion in own grounds on the south coast of England. Surrounded by lawns, trees and beautiful gardens.
8 North London: 2-bedroomed modernised terraced house with large lounge, modern kitchen. Garage at back of house.

2 Read the following letter. In your exercise book write the missing word after each number.

Dear Lola,

Our (1) _____ has a lovely view. It is on the fifth (2) _____ in a small, modern (3) _____ of flats. It is very pleasant to sit out on the (4) _____ on a nice day and look at the view. Fortunately, it is only a six- (5) _____ building, and so we are almost at the top. However, my best friend lives on the (6) _____ floor, and there is a lovely (7) _____ full of trees and flowers outside his front door. At the back there are several (8) _____ , and we can keep our car in one of them.

You told me you lived in a semi- (9) _____ bungalow on the outskirts of Madrid. Do you stay at (10) _____ most evenings or do you go out a lot? Please write and tell me more about yourself.

Yours truly,

Diana Witton

3 Listen to the conversation on the tape. If you agree with a statement, write YES after the number of the statement. If you do not agree, write NO.

1 The man thinks flats have better views than houses.
2 His wife thinks that a lot of houses are built like prisons.
3 Her husband enjoys gardening.
4 Their children would enjoy running about and playing more if they lived in a flat.
5 The man thinks that flats are safer than houses, especially when you are away on holiday.
6 The man thinks that flats are a lot quieter than houses.
7 His wife agrees with him.
8 The man and the woman live in a house at present.

4 Work in pairs.

Look at the following notices and then discuss them with your partner. Try to guess where you would see each of them and what it means.

BREAK GLASS in case of fire	Lift out of order Use stairs	· TO LET · Small furnished apartment
Ring bell number of times shown by stars: Ericsson* Sanchez*** Law** Faoud****	EMERGENCY EXIT	SERVICE ENTRANCE and all deliveries at back

5 Look at the pictures of the house described in the advertisement below. Then write a short paragraph giving a *true* description of the house.

FOR SALE Large detached house with lovely views of beautiful countryside. Suitable for big family. Excellent position near shops and railway station; also within walking distance of the beach. Four air-conditioned bedrooms (two with attached bathrooms), large modern kitchen, pleasant lounge, and dining-room. All rooms are large and comfortable with good furniture. Set in large garden with swimming pool. Large garage: well-built but needs slight repairs.

DINING ROOM

LOUNGE

KITCHEN

6 Finish the second sentence in each pair so that it has the same meaning as the first sentence. Write out the complete sentence in your exercise book.

EXAMPLE:

Our flat has two bedrooms.

There *are two bedrooms in our flat.* _____ .

A NECESSITY

1 How many rooms in the flat must we paint?
   How many rooms in the flat is it _____ ?
2 It isn't necessary for you to paint every room.
   You don't _____ .

B POSSIBILITY

3 We can rent the flat on the top floor.
   It's possible for _____ .
4 It's impossible for me to buy such an expensive flat.
   I _____ .

C COMPARISON

5 Yoko's flat is larger than Midori's.
   Midori's _____ .
6 There isn't a nicer flat in our neighbourhood than yours.
   Your flat _____ .

D CLAUSES

7 Before you start to paint the room, cover all the chairs and the sofa.
   After _____ .
8 I like this flat in spite of the noisy neighbourhood _____ .
   Although _____ .

E REPORTED SPEECH

9 'I'm going to fit new locks on all the doors,' Sarah said.
   Sarah said that _____ .
10 'Don't buy a big house in the country,' Manuel said to us.
   Manuel told us _____ .

F PASSIVE VOICE

11 You should repair the broken window as soon as possible.
   The broken window _____ .
12 They've built a new house nearby.
   A new house _____ .

7 Here are some sentences about a flat. Finish the second sentence in each pair so that it has the same meaning as the first. Write out the complete sentence in your exercise book.

1 Each of the rooms in my new flat has an excellent view.
   There is _____ .
2 The flats on the lower floors are not as nice as this flat.
   This flat _____ .
3 A lot are too small for large families to live in comfortably.
   A lot aren't _____ .
4 It isn't even necessary to clean outside the flat.
   You don't _____ .
5 The owners of the flats employ a cleaner and two guards.
   A cleaner _____ .
6 Unfortunately, most ordinary people cannot afford to rent a flat here.
   Unfortunately, few _____ .
7 Nevertheless, in spite of the high rents, all the flats have been taken.
   Nevertheless, although _____ .
8 The neighbourhood is very popular with businessmen.
   Businessmen _____ .

Health

1 What's wrong?

Match each picture with the appropriate illness. Then put the appropriate remedy with the illness. Write only letters and numbers.

EXAMPLE:
  (A – 6 – iii)

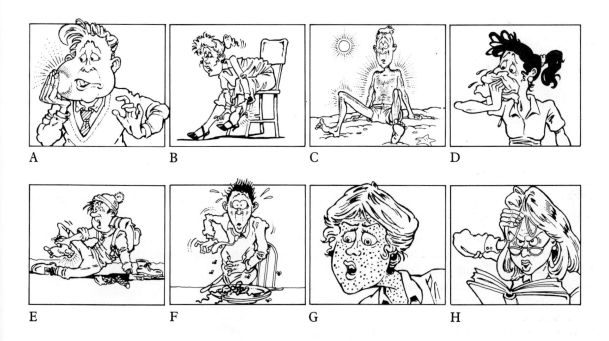

1 'My nose won't stop bleeding.'
2 'I think I've got measles.'
3 'I can't walk. I think I've sprained my ankle.'
4 'I've got a splitting headache.'
5 'These blisters are very painful when I walk.'
6 'Oh dear, I've got very bad toothache.'
7 'I can't eat any more. I feel sick.'
8 'I've got sunburnt quite badly. It's very painful.'

i) 'Sit over here in the shade and put this wet towel over yourself.'
ii) 'Stop reading at once and take one of these tablets. Then have a rest and close your eyes for a few minutes.'
iii) 'Why don't you see a dentist?'
iv) 'Have a drink of water and don't eat so much in future.'
v) 'Take off your shoe and sock at once and put your foot in some cold water.'
vi) 'Bend your head forward over a bowl and try breathing through your mouth. If it doesn't stop bleeding after a few minutes, see a doctor.'
vii) 'Go to the doctor's at once.'
viii) 'Prick them with a clean needle and then put a plaster over them.'

2 Work in small groups. One student in each group should pretend to be a dentist's receptionist. He/She should look at the dentist's diary on page 117 and should help other students in the group to make a suitable appointment. *The other students should not look at the diary.* Imagine that today is Monday.

The other students in the group should take it in turns to telephone the dentist's receptionist and make an appointment at one of these times:

1 as soon as possible (bad toothache)
2 any time before half-past nine: the sooner the better
3 any time except between nine and eleven or between twelve and one
4 any time on Saturday morning
5 between quarter to eleven and quarter to one on Tuesday or Wednesday
6 as late in the morning as possible on Friday
7 as early in the morning as possible on Thursday or Friday
8 as soon as possible any morning after eleven o'clock

EXAMPLE:

STUDENT A:	Could I make an appointment, please?
RECEPTIONIST:	Certainly. Can you come at ten o'clock today?
STUDENT A:	I'm sorry. I've got another appointment then. Could I come tomorrow morning?
RECEPTIONIST:	Yes, you can have an appointment tomorrow morning at nine thirty.
STUDENT A:	Thank you. That'll be fine.
RECEPTIONIST:	What's your name, please?
STUDENT A:	Alamiri. Carlos Alamiri.

3 Complete the conversation between Tony Small and a shop assistant and write out the completed conversation in your exercise book. Two years ago Tony bought some bathroom scales to weigh himself regularly. Unfortunately, the scales are no longer accurate. Tony has taken them to the shop where he bought them and would like to have them repaired.

SHOP ASSISTANT:	Good afternoon. Can I help you?
TONY SMALL:	_____

SHOP ASSISTANT:	I think we can. It shouldn't be too big a job.
TONY SMALL:	_____
SHOP ASSISTANT:	A week on Saturday. They should be ready then.
TONY SMALL:	_____
SHOP ASSISTANT:	I can't say until we look at them. It'll probably be about £10.
TONY SMALL:	_____
SHOP ASSISTANT:	Can you let me have your name and phone number, please?
TONY SMALL:	_____
SHOP ASSISTANT:	This is a receipt for the scales. Thank you very much, sir.

4 Work in pairs.

STUDENT A:
Turn to page 118.

STUDENT B:
You work in a shop which sells exercise machines and other equipment for gymnasiums. Ask Student A what is wrong with the machine he has brought back and how long he has had it. Try to find out if he has broken it through rough use or if there was a fault in the machine.

5 First, copy out the following notes. Then listen to the conversation between Dr Lee and Alison. Imagine that you are Dr Lee. Put a tick in the boxes you think are the most suitable and then complete the notes.

1
Earache	Headache	Stomach ache	Cough

2
Feels sick	Feels dizzy	Feels faint

3 Temperature
YES	NO

4 How long ago illness started: _____
5 Cause: _____
6 Medicine to be taken: How many tablets _____
　　　　　　　　　　　　　How often _____
　　　　　　　　　　　　　For how long _____

6 How long will you live?

Read the following sentences. Write the numbers of only those sentences which are TRUE for you.

1 I like doing difficult but interesting things.
2 Sometimes every small problem seems like a very big problem.
3 For some reason or other, I'm often unlucky.
4 I always talk about my problems to some of my friends.
5 I feel I can never tell my friends about my problems: they don't seem to understand.
6 I never show my anger to other people.
7 When I am angry or upset, I usually play a game.
8 I'd like to have a change and go away for a long holiday.
9 I play games fairly often.
10 I never play games but I know I should do some exercise.
11 I can never sit still and do nothing.
12 I often feel tired.
13 I always laugh when I hear a good joke.
14 Life is very serious, and I don't laugh much.
15 I often have a bad cough.
16 I like eating a lot of sweets and chocolate.
17 I never feel very hungry.
18 I often eat too much.
19 I am keen on reading a lot.
20 I can put my books away and forget about my work whenever I want to.

GOOD NUMBERS: 1, 4, 7, 9, 13, 19, 20
You should feel happy if you have written down four or more of these numbers. Your choice of these numbers will help you to live longer.

DANGEROUS HABITS: 10, 11, 16, 18
The sentences with these numbers describe habits which may cause you harm. You should try to change these habits. I hope you have not chosen two or more of these numbers.

SERIOUS SIGNS: 2, 3, 5, 6, 8, 14
You should learn to relax and take a rest if you have written down two or more of these numbers.

SEE A DOCTOR: 12, 15, 17
If you have written down even ONE of these numbers, you should see a doctor. A visit to the doctor now may help you a lot.

7 Work in pairs.

STUDENT A:
Turn to page 118.

STUDENT B:
Listen to what Student A says about a new health and fitness club. However, you are very busy most evenings this week. Try to find an evening when you can go with Student A. (You are quite keen on swimming.) *Do NOT look at the notice on page 118.*

A

UNIT SIX

The Weather

1 Work in pairs.

STUDENT A:
   Look at MAP A below and then complete as much as possible of the table in this section.
   Next exchange information orally with your partner. In this way, you should both help each other to complete the table which follows *without looking at each other's map.*

STUDENT B:
   Turn to page 118.

TODAY'S WEATHER
MAP A (ONLY Student A should look at this map.)

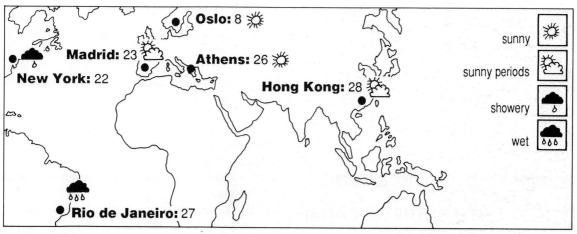

CITY	TEMP	WEATHER	CITY	TEMP	WEATHER
Athens			Mexico City		
Cairo			New York		
			Oslo		
Hong Kong			Rio de Janeiro		
London			Rome		
			Tokyo		

Now answer these questions.

1 Which is the hottest city?
2 Which city has the lowest temperature?
3 In which cities will it rain?
4 What is the weather like in London today?
5 Which city do you think has the best weather today?

2 Look at the following five notices. Someone asks you what each notice means. For each notice write out the letter (A, B, C or D) of the correct answer.

1

ARSENAL v BARCELONA
Kick-off 3pm
CANCELLED
OWING TO HEAVY RAIN

A The match will start as soon as it stops raining.
B There will be no match as a result of the rain.
C The match will take place as planned in spite of the heavy rain.
D The match will now begin at three o'clock unless it rains heavily.

2

Arrival of all flights
DELAYED
as a result of fog

A All planes will land at another airport owing to fog.
B Fog is making it difficult for planes to take off on time.
C Because it is foggy, all planes will arrive late.
D Fog has made it necessary to cancel all flights.

3

Ice and snow ahead
DRIVE WITH EXTREME CARE!

A Drive very carefully because ice and snow have made the road dangerous.
B Ice and snow are now being cleared away from the road.
C You cannot drive any further because there is ice and snow on the road.
D Drivers helping to remove ice and snow from the road should be very careful.

4

RIO DE JANEIRO
Yesterday's temperatures
Max. 24°C   Min. 16°C

A The temperature was only 16°C yesterday.
B The temperature rose to more than 24°C yesterday.
C The temperature fell to less than 16°C yesterday.
D The temperature did not reach higher than 24°C yesterday.

5

TODAY'S WEATHER

Clear skies at first
but showers
developing

A It will be very sunny everywhere all day.
B Later today there will be rain at times in certain places.
C The rain will soon stop, and it will become bright and sunny.
D Clouds and rain will be replaced by clear skies.

3 Read the following weather report and write the letter of the word which best fits each space.

Today there will be a northerly wind over the whole of the country (1) _____ it will not be very strong. Consequently, it should feel quite (2) _____ when the sun shines. (3) _____ there will be some pleasant sunny (4) _____ over the north of the country, the south will have some showers later in the afternoon. The eastern parts of the country, however, will have another dull day with outbreaks of (5) _____ .

The (6) _____ for tomorrow is very good. (7) _____ a few showers during the night, there will be fairly long periods of (8) _____ over most of the country.

1	A	so	B	for	C	but	D	because
2	A	warm	B	cool	C	cold	D	dry
3	A	But	B	However	C	Because	D	Although
4	A	times	B	periods	C	breaks	D	hours
5	A	sun	B	cloud	C	rain	D	warmth
6	A	outlook	B	hope	C	plan	D	future
7	A	Before	B	When	C	As soon as	D	After
8	A	sunshine	B	clouds	C	showers	D	flooding

4 Copy out the following boxes. Then listen to the weather forecast on the tape. While you are listening, put a tick in either ONE box or TWO boxes for each day. Finally, write down (1) today's maximum temperature and (2) today's minimum temperature.

	YESTERDAY	TODAY	TOMORROW
Fog			
Rain			
Snow			
Sunshine			

5 Work in pairs.

STUDENT A:

You plan to go on business trips next year to Delhi and Rio de Janeiro. However, you don't know much about the climate in these cities. Ask Student B to advise you about the best times to go and the kind of weather there.

STUDENT B:

Turn to page 119.

STUDENT A:

Now turn to page 119 and answer Student B's questions.

STUDENT B:

Stop looking at the climate guide and ask Student A about the best time of the year to pay a visit to Hong Kong. You would like to combine your business trip with a short holiday in Hong Kong. You are fond of swimming, sunbathing and sightseeing. You also wonder about making a trip to Melbourne immediately after your Hong Kong visit.

6 Read the following and write the letter (A, B, C or D) of the word which best fits each space.

Dear Anna,

Last week a typhoon struck Hong Kong. When we first heard that it was coming towards us, the (1)____ was very hot and (2)____ . The sky was (3)____ and it was very (4)____ . I didn't believe the weather (5)____ on the radio: I thought they had made a mistake. Later that day, however, clouds appeared and it quickly (6)____ cooler. Then the (7)____ became stronger throughout the night and several trees were (8)____ down. That night was the worst night of my life.

When morning came, it was suddenly very (9)____ : we were at the centre of the typhoon! An hour or two later the wind started again, but it was not quite as (10)____ as before. Nevertheless, there was a lot of damage, and a number of people were killed.

I shall write again to you when we have fully recovered from this terrible typhoon.

Love,
Della.

1	A	temperature	B	weather	C	sky	D	climate
2	A	dry	B	dried	C	drying	D	dryly
3	A	straight	B	empty	C	deep	D	clear
4	A	sun	B	sunny	C	sunlight	D	sunshine
5	A	article	B	forecast	C	announcement	D	story
6	A	became	B	seemed	C	felt	D	blew
7	A	rain	B	coolness	C	wind	D	temperature
8	A	knocked	B	pushed	C	turned	D	blown
9	A	easy	B	weak	C	calm	D	gentle
10	A	big	B	strong	C	high	D	steep

UNIT SEVEN

Transport

1 Look at the following timetable and then choose the best word from the list below it.

Sevilla	0720	0815	0902	1037	1115	1350	1530	1630	1730
Utrera	0758	0854	0940	1115	1153	1431	1608	1711	1808
Marchena	0812	0908			1207		1622	1725	
Osuna		0918						1737	
Estepa	0830	0930	1012	1147	1225	1500	1640	1749	1840

never	seldom	sometimes	generally	always

1 The trains from Sevilla to Estepa _____ stop at Osuna.
2 The trains _____ stop at Marchena.
3 You can _____ catch the Estepa train at Utrera.
4 It _____ takes longer than one hour and twenty minutes to travel from Sevilla to Estepa.
5 The trains from Sevilla _____ reach Estepa in one hour and ten minutes.

2 Work in pairs.

STUDENT A:
   Look at the plan of the London Underground in this section and answer Student B's questions.

STUDENT B:
   Do NOT look at the plan and ask Student A how to get:

      from Charing Cross to Oxford Circus
      from Knightsbridge to Bond Street
      from Bayswater to Piccadilly Circus
      from St Paul's to King's Cross

STUDENT B:
   Now look at the plan of the London Underground and answer Student A's questions.
STUDENT A:
   Do NOT look at the plan and ask Student B how to get:

from Baker Street to Green Park
from Leicester Square to Bond Street
from Hyde Park Corner to Farringdon
from Holborn to Victoria

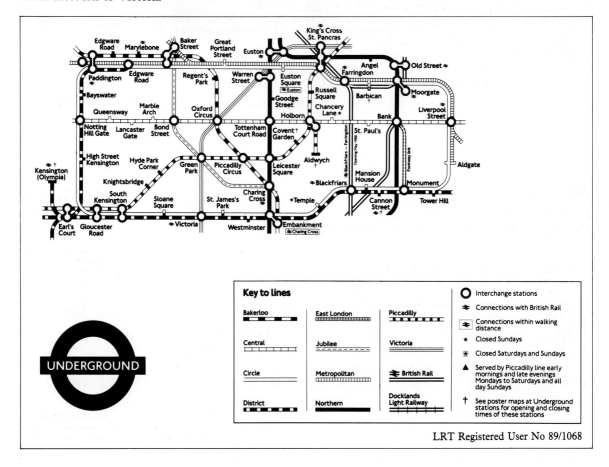

LRT Registered User No 89/1068

3 Read the following information about rail tickets as quickly as you can. Who can be the first to answer the question below?

When can't you use saver tickets?

RAIL TICKETS

Single from Leeds to Manchester: £4
Ordinary return from Leeds to Manchester: £7.20
Cheap day return from Leeds to Manchester: £5.80
Saver: £5.40*
Season: 1 week   £24.50
        1 month   £94
        3 months   £256

*Note: Valid for 3 months except on trains departing from Leeds between 7.15 am and 8.45 am and departing from Manchester between 4.30 pm and 6.00 pm Mondays to Fridays.

Now read the information once again. Write the numbers of those sentences which you think are correct.

1 A cheap day return is a rail ticket which can be used only if you are going to make the return journey on the same day.
2 A saver ticket costs less than a cheap day return.
3 A saver ticket can be used for a return journey at any time of the day during the weekend but only at certain times of the day during the week.
4 An ordinary return ticket is the same price as two single tickets.
5 If you travel from Leeds to Manchester and back every day from Monday to Friday, it is cheaper to buy a cheap day return every day than a season ticket for a week.
6 You can use saver tickets on the quarter past eight train from Leeds to Manchester on Wednesday mornings.

4 Look at the following timetable showing the coach services from Brisbane Coach Station. Then look at the map at the side of the timetable. Listen carefully to the tape. Then write T (= True) or F (= False) after the number of each part of the conversation.

Ipswich	Gympie	Toowoomba	Southport
6.30*	9.10	11.45	8.12
8.00	11.10	6.00	8.42*
9.15	1.10	8.15*	9.12
10.30	3.10		9.42*
11.45	5.10		10.12
12.30	7.10		12.12
2.15			1.12
3.45			4.12
6.00			5.42*
8.15			6.12
			8.24*

Note: ★ = Not on Sunday

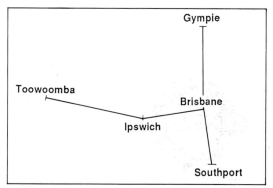

1 _____   2 _____   3 _____
4 _____   5 _____   6 _____

5 Work in pairs.

STUDENT A:
  Look at the incomplete plan. It shows the places to which trains travel from Tokyo. It also shows the times taken to travel to these places. Ask Student B questions and also answer his/her questions so that you can complete your plans. However, do NOT look at each other's plans.

STUDENT B:
  Turn to page 119.

Only Student A should look at this.

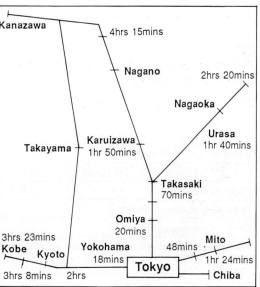

After completing your plans, both of you should answer the following questions.

1 How much longer does it take to travel to Taira than to Mito?
2 Which two cities take almost three hours to reach from Tokyo?
3 Which city takes the longest to reach from Tokyo on this map?
4 Which cities or towns do you pass through to reach Kobe?
5 Is it possible to travel from Tokyo to Kanazawa via Takayama?
6 Which is the faster route to Toyama?

6 First, copy the table below into your exercise book. You are at Madrid Airport. The airport announcements are being given first in Spanish and then in English. Listen to the airport announcements in English on the tape. As you listen, complete the information about the departures below.

NOTE: In the information column write one of the following words:

Departed Boarding Postponed Cancelled

However, leave any space blank if no announcement is made.

Dep Time	Flight No.	Destination	Information	Gate
10.35	CU146	Havana	Departed	3
10.40	BA361		Boarding	
10.45		Cairo		
10.50	A1621			8
10.50		Athens	Boarding	
10.55	IB132			
11.00	JL718			7
11.05			Cancelled	
11.05		New York		
11.10		Buenos Aires		3

7 First, copy the form below into your exercise book. You have travelled on Flight KLM 426 to Rio de Janeiro leaving Montevideo at 11.10 on January 15th and arriving in Rio at 14.00. You are now in Rio but one of your cases (shown in the picture) is missing. Complete this form so that the airline can look for it.

When did you arrive in Rio de Janeiro?	
Where did you travel from?	
How did you travel? Air / Sea / Road * (*Circle as appropriate)	
Flight no/Name of ship	
Description of baggage lost	
Details of contents	
Value of contents	
Signature	Date

8

Listen to the travel report on the radio. Look at the following notes and write the letter or letters (A, B, C or D) which you think is the most suitable.

1 Road conditions

A Floods

B Ice

C Snow

D Fog

2 Motorways

A M1

B M6

C M25

D M62

3 British Rail

A Southern Region

B Northern Region

C Western Region

D Eastern Region

4 Underground

A Piccadilly Line

B Circle Line

C Victoria Line

D Bakerloo Line

5 Ferries

A Dunkirk

B Calais

C Boulogne

D St. Malo

6 Flights

A Britain

B Europe

C Middle East

D Far East

UNIT EIGHT

Schools and Colleges

1 Work in small groups.

Some people think the following statements describe a good school. Which three of these statements do you think are the most important for a good school? Discuss your choices and your reasons.

1 The school lets pupils leave when they don't have lessons.
2 The school rules are very strict and the school punishes pupils who come late and are often absent.
3 The school has some excellent teachers who know a lot about their subjects.
4 The school is very good at preparing pupils for examinations, especially for entrance to universities and colleges.
5 The teachers spend a lot of time with the weaker pupils.
6 Games and sports are very important in the school.
7 Most of the teachers always set pupils a very good example.
8 The school has a lot of clubs and societies for pupils.
9 There are a lot of excursions and interesting visits for pupils.
10 Most of the staff and pupils at the school seem very friendly and happy.
11 Pupils respect their teachers and always obey the school rules.
12 The school is very modern and has very good classrooms.

2 Which word best completes each blank in the following paragraph? Write out the paragraph, replacing each blank with the most suitable word.

lesson	subject	course	syllabus	timetable

The (1) _____ in which I got the best results in my last examinations was English. In our college we have an English (2) _____ every day: in the class (3) _____ it is usually the first or second period every morning. Other languages which are taught in my college are German, Spanish and Arabic. The English (4) _____ includes not only the English language but also English life and customs. Next year I would like to take an English (5) _____ at a summer school in Britain.

3 Read the paragraph below and then try to complete the timetable.

The subject which Sue likes best is History, but she likes English and Geography a lot, too. English is the first subject on her timetable each day apart from Tuesday. She has Maths lessons in the second period on Monday and Thursday mornings as well as in the third period on both Tuesday and Wednesday mornings. Her Physics lesson occupies a double period on Monday morning. However, this is followed by her favourite subject in the afternoon. She likes Tuesdays better than Mondays because she has Geography before the mid-morning break and also Physical Education at the end of the morning. The last period on Tuesday afternoons is Music, another subject she enjoys. Wednesday afternoons are very popular as the class has Games – usually basketball or hockey. Spanish is taught every day and there is a double period of Art on Thursday afternoons. There is also a double period of Biology on Friday mornings, one period before the mid-morning break and one after it.

	9.00 – 9.40	9.40 – 10.20		10.40 – 11.20	11.20 – 12.00		1.30 – 2.10	2.10 – 2.50	2.50 – 3.30
MON		Maths	K			H		Spanish	Biology
TUES	Spanish		A			C	Civics	English	
WED	English	Chem	E		History	N	Spanish		
THURS	English		R	Chem		U	Geog		
FRI	English		B		English	L	History		Civics

4 Can you fill in a form?

Using the information in the letter below, complete the following application form for a bus pass.

Dear Sir,
I wish to apply for a pass to travel by bus to my college. My name is Helen Susan Clifford and I go to New Method Girls' College in Newley. I was born on 17th October, 1976 and I live at 172 Reardon Drive, Causeway Bay, Newley. I want to travel on a Number 73 or 82 bus from Foster Square to the Odeon Cinema halfway down Lawnswood Road (opposite New Method College) each morning and back home at the end of each afternoon.

I do hope you will send me a bus pass as soon as possible.

Yours faithfully,

H S Clifford

Surname	Other names
Date of Birth	Sex: Male/Female*
Home Address	
Name of School	
Address	
Route No.	
Journey: Single/Return* Between and	
Signature	Date

5 First, copy out the notes below. Then listen to the tape recording of a radio programme called *Education Today*. You will hear details and comments about a school of English. Write the missing information in your notes and put a tick in the boxes you think are most suitable.

Name of school: _____

Length of courses: _____

Age group(s):   Under 17 ☐   17–21 ☐   Over 21 ☐

Type of courses: General English   ☐   Holiday English   ☐

               Business English   ☐   Technical English   ☐

               Medical English   ☐   Study Skills   ☐

Class size: _____   Number of hours weekly: _____

Language laboratory: ☐   Video: ☐   Library: ☐   Computers: ☐

Fees: _____

Put a tick in the box if the fees include: accommodation   ☐

                                    excursions   ☐

Type of accommodation: Family ☐   School ☐   Hotel ☐

Other activities: _____

6 Work in small groups. (Preferably four to five students should be in each group.)

STUDENT A:
You work in an education office in your country. Turn to pages 119 and 120.

STUDENTS B, C, D AND E should pretend to be one of the people listed below.

STUDENT B:
You are a businessman living in Mexico City and you want to go to Britain to improve your English skills for your job. You can stay only one month in Britain, and you want the best course available. Phone up your local education office to ask for advice. Remember to ask about fees and accommodation.

STUDENT C:
You now want to arrange an English course for a party of six children. You want advice on the best place for this purpose as well as details about fees, accommodation, activities, etc.

STUDENT D:

You want to teach English either in your country or in a neighbouring country. You want to get a good qualification. Ask for advice about a course in Britain, the length of the course, the cost, the place, etc.

STUDENT E:

A friend of yours wants his son to go to England for a month's holiday. His son is fond of sports and games, but he does not want to spend all the time learning English in a language school. Phone up the education office on behalf of your friend and ask for their advice (and all necessary details).

7 You wish to apply to take an English language course at one of the schools or colleges listed on pages 119 and 120. Choose whichever school or college you would like to attend. Complete the following application form, giving details about yourself.

APPLICATION FOR COURSE

Full name _____ Mr/Mrs/Miss

Nationality _____ Age _____

Address in your country _____

_____

_____

Place of study in your country _____

Exams already passed _____

What do you think is your level of English?   (Circle the most appropriate level below.)

   Beginner / Lower Intermediate / Intermediate / Upper Intermediate / Advanced

What do you find most difficult in English? _____

_____

What is your reason for wanting to study in Britain? _____

_____

Why have you chosen this particular school/college? _____

_____

What else do you hope to do during your stay in Britain? _____

_____

Is there any food which you cannot eat? _____

_____

Signature _____ Date _____

UNIT NINE

People

1 Listen to the short conversations on tape. Can you guess which name goes with which picture?

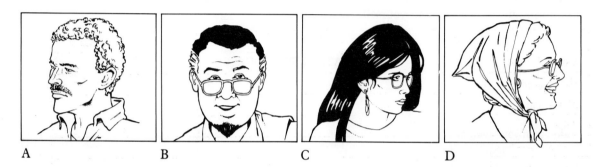

A   B   C   D

2 Read about the following characteristics of people born in certain years. The information is from a book on Chinese horoscopes and it describes people's personalities according to the year of their birth. Each year is represented by an animal. For example, anybody born between January 16, 1972 and February 2, 1973 is a Rat; anybody born between January 23, 1974 and February 10, 1975 is a Tiger.

Don't try to understand every word and don't use a dictionary!

The charm of the Rat's personality is universally known. On the surface, he seems to be quiet, pleasant, and well-balanced, but don't be deceived! Beneath this calm exterior, there is hidden aggression: the Rat can become very angry and rude when he is upset. If you stay with the Rat for a while, you will discover how nervous and quick-tempered he can be.

In the East, the Tiger is a symbol of strength, passion and daring. The Tiger loves to rebel and find fault with things. He is full of confidence and he will always be the leader at the centre of any trouble. Be careful before you follow him or you may find yourself heading for danger.

The Rabbit symbolises good manners, sound advice and kindness. The Rabbit can usually get his way without having to argue. He dislikes quarrels and fights, and he will never deliberately upset people or go out of his way to criticise anyone.

Although the Snake has a bad reputation in the West, he is respected for his wisdom and goodwill in the East. Men born under the sign of the Snake are charming and have a sense of humour. Women born under this sign are usually beautiful and successful. The Snake always relies on his own judgement and doesn't communicate well with others.

The Horse has an independent spirit and is an adventurer at heart. He loves exercise and he is usually a great sportsman. You can easily spot the Horse by his graceful movements. He is hot-blooded, hot-headed and impatient. He expects people to do things quickly and he is unhappy if they are not as quick and efficient as he is.

You should be able to guess the personality of anyone born under the sign of the Monkey. He will be mischievous, playful and full of fun, of course. Although he's a very sociable creature, the Monkey is also very selfish and vain. The Monkey is intelligent and can solve the most difficult problems.

Which animal signs are most suitable for the persons described in the following sentences?
Write the name of only one sign for each person.

1 I've never heard Estella Vargas arguing with anyone or saying anything bad about anyone.
2 I can't understand Ken Mitsumo. Although we work closely together, he usually makes up his own mind without listening to me or anyone else. Then he does things without telling me about them.
3 Maria Da Silva loves to play little jokes on people and tease them. A lot of people think she's not very intelligent, but they're wrong. She is very clever indeed.
4 Ali Ahmad is such a quiet person and he's always very calm. So you can imagine my surprise when he suddenly began to shout at the bus conductor and shake his fist at him.
5 Although Stefan Fotos is an excellent tennis player, he's not a very good teacher. I think he is far too impatient with beginners, and I wouldn't like to take lessons from him.
6 Sheila Scott persuaded her workmates to refuse to work longer hours and said she would see the boss to complain.

	Rat	Tiger	Rabbit	Snake	Horse	Monkey
Estella Vargas						
Ken Mitsumo						
Maria Da Silva						
Ali Ahmad						
Stefan Fotos						
Sheila Scott						

NOTE: If you want to know which animal sign you are, your teacher has the information in the Teacher's Guide.

3 You have taken the following notes from a book about Chinese horoscopes. Write a short paragraph describing someone who is a Dragon.

Dragon = healthy and strong
energetic - fire from mouth!
always wants the best
big mouth and big heart
gives good advice
intelligent, always confident, can do anything
strong temper
generous, always loyal to family when needed

Begin your paragraph:

In China the Dragon is a sign of power. People who are born in the year of the Dragon ....

4 Read these paragraphs and then answer the questions which follow. Write only the letter of the correct answer in Questions 1 and 2. Then write your answers to Questions 3, 4 and 5 in your exercise book.

A day in the life of Steve Bowen, the famous writer

The alarm goes off at quarter past six every morning. The ringing seems to go straight through my head. I reach out and switch the alarm off. For two or three minutes I lie in bed in that unhappy state between sleeping and waking. At last I swing my feet out of bed.

My wife is a doctor and, when she has been on duty late the previous night, I take her a cup of tea. Then I make breakfast for the family – my wife Annabella and our three children Derek, Tina and Susan. My wife leaves home at eight precisely and is never late for her surgery. I take the children to school in the old family car.

I am usually back home by nine and then I start work. At first people used to call and see me. They thought that a writer had time to talk for as long as anyone cared to stay. Now they know not to call between nine and three every day.

I take a large cup of coffee to my desk and sit down at my word processor. Writing is always hard work, but I make myself sit and write. The room where I work has no view. I have arranged this deliberately so that I do not waste time gazing out of the window. I write through the lunch hour until three o'clock in the afternoon. Then I have a sandwich and a cup of tea before picking up the children from school.

My wife arrives home by six but she sometimes has to go out again to visit her patients. She goes out whenever anyone telephones – even when she thinks the person probably isn't very ill. While she is out, I usually help the children with their homework or watch television. As soon as she returns, she always makes us a cup of coffee and gives us a snack no matter how tired she may be.

From nine o'clock until midnight, however, I sit down again at my word processor and I work for three hours. I do this every night except Saturday. On Saturday my wife and I go out to a cinema and then to our favourite disco. We make the most of our night out and we enjoy every minute of it!

---

1 These paragraphs are from
   A a novel.   B a letter.   C a newspaper article.   D an advertisement.

2 The writer seems to be a person who
   A is easily persuaded to do things.   B is hard-working and determined to succeed
   C likes to have a comfortable life and talk to his friends.
   D is rather lazy and likes other people to work for him.

3 The writer has planned his room so that _____ .

4 The writer's wife has to spend some evenings _____ .

5 How do the writer and his wife like to spend their leisure time?

5 Work in pairs.

STUDENT A:
   Turn to page 120.

STUDENT B:
   Listen to Student A describe the photograph which he/she is looking at. Ask any questions you want about it. Try to form as clear a picture as you can of A's photograph. Finally, look at A's photograph. In what way is it different from what you expected? How could A have described it more accurately?

   Now look at the photograph on page 65. Talk about it to Student A.

Remember to describe
  the boy's faces
  their clothes and general appearance
  what they are doing
  what they may be thinking
  any other important details in the picture

Only Student B should look at this photograph.

6   Work in pairs.

STUDENT B:

Turn to page 120.

STUDENT A:

Look at the photograph and talk about it to Student B. Listen to Student B talk about his/her photograph and try to find out how the two photographs are similar and how they are different. Later, show Student B your photograph and discuss the two photographs.

Only Student A should look at this photograph.

UNIT TEN

Holidays

1 Work in small groups.

What would you take with you on holiday to a small island in the Pacific Ocean? It is a very beautiful island and there are two mountains and a small lake. There are some rare birds and one or two strange animals. The capital of the island is very small, but there are two modern hotels, each with a swimming pool, tennis courts, and a golf course. There are some beautiful beaches on the island and a lot of people go swimming, sailing and water skiing. There is little to do in the capital but the island is excellent for walking and cycling.

You should write out the following items in the order which you prefer.

When you have done this, you should discuss your answers with other members of the group and give reasons for your choice. The students in the group should see how much they agree with one another.

Finally, discuss what items are missing from the list. What do you suggest should be on the list?

Some good books
A tennis racquet
Some walking shoes
A bathing costume/Some swimming trunks
A cassette radio
A camera
Some puzzles
Some medicine for a bad stomach
Some golf clubs
Some board games (eg chess)

2 Which words do not belong in each group? Write out the word which is different from the other three words in the set. Then say or write *why* you think the word is the odd one in the set.

1	trip	excursion	tour	hotel
2	scenery	countryside	attraction	landscape
3	relax	rest	work	play
4	tourist	holidaymaker	visitor	inhabitant
5	island	beach	shore	coast
6	clothes	luggage	bags	cases

3 Listen to the information on the tape about holidays in Tunisia. Then copy out the following table and complete it. Next, write out the list of facilities which the hotels have. Put a tick in each column, as appropriate. Finally, complete the sentences in Question 3.

1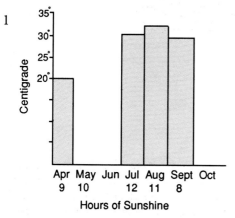

2

	Samar	Neptune
Swimming pool		
Children's playground		
Children's pool		
Golf course		
Tennis courts		
Surfing		
Sailing		
Bar		
Videos		
Discos		

3 (a) The Samar Hotel is suitable for _____

(b) The Hotel Neptune is suitable for _____

4 Read the following advertisement. Imagine that you have chosen Crete for a holiday. Write a short letter to a friend telling him or her about your holiday plans and the reasons for choosing to go to Crete.

COME

TO

SUNNY

CRETE!

Crete is the perfect island for those who want sunbathing, swimming and fascinating sightseeing.

You can see the remains of Europe's first civilisation. The most famous place to visit is the Palace of Knossos, where King Minos ruled more than three thousand years ago.

The present-day capital, Heraklion, is one of the most interesting towns in the Mediterranean. You will be fasci-nated by the old walls round the town, the beautiful and ancient castle, and the busy harbour. Heraklion is also an excellent place for shopping and dining.

Take some of the many interesting excursions from Heraklion and you will see beautiful valleys, dramatic cliffs, and interesting caves as well as miles and miles of clean sandy beaches.

5 Look at the route on the map and read the description of a coach tour from England to Switzerland. The description has been taken from a holiday guide.

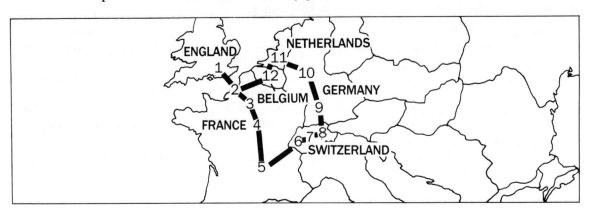

We cross to Calais from Dover by ferry and drive to Lille for our first overnight stay. Early the following morning we drive to Paris to spend the rest of the morning there before continuing south in the afternoon. We arrive in the early evening at Macon, where we stay at the Hotel Frantel. The next day our route takes us through the mountains of Jura to reach Lausanne in Switzerland. Following the shore of Lake Geneva, we reach Villars, a ski resort with beautiful mountain views. The next two days are spent exploring Villars and the surrounding countryside. Refreshed by our short stay, we then drive across Switzerland to Davos, where we stay at the Hotel Sunstar. Davos is a famous health resort in the eastern part of Switzerland, surrounded by magnificent forests. On the following day we leave Davos and enter Germany through the Black Forest and on to Mannheim. After continuing north through the wooded Taunus Hills, we visit Cologne before arriving in the old town of Ghent in the Netherlands for our final overnight stay. We leave early in the morning for a quick visit to the beautiful old town of Bruges and then on to Calais to catch the ferry back to Dover.

Now write down each number followed by the appropriate place which the people on the coach visited. Put a circle round the names of those places where they stayed overnight.

6 Flights from London to Spain and Portugal

SUPERSAVE FARES

	Mon – Thurs	Fri – Sun
Barcelona	£183	£213
Lisbon	£210	£240

Length of stay: 6 days to 1 month
Booking date: At least 2 weeks before departure
Stops on the way: None
Cancellation: No refund
Reduction for children: Infants under 2 (sharing parent's seat) pay £25 each

EUROSAVE FARES

Barcelona	£252
Lisbon	£280

Length of stay: 1 night to 6 months
Booking date: Any time
Stops on the way: One stop allowed
Cancellation: Full refund if 1 week before departure
Reduction for children: Children 2 to 11 pay 50% of adult fare
Infants under 2 (sharing parent's seat) pay 10% of adult fare

Now read the following information about people who are going to Barcelona and Lisbon by air. What is the smallest amount which they need to pay? Write the correct amount after the number of each sentence.

1 Mr and Mrs Binns want to spend three weeks in Barcelona. Today is Saturday and they want to leave in exactly one month.
2 Mr Sato is attending a business conference in Lisbon for three days and wants to book a flight leaving London the day after tomorrow, Tuesday September 5th.
3 Mr and Mrs Lee are going to spend from November to February in Lisbon. They can travel on any day of the week.
4 Vincent Pomeroy is going on a three-week holiday to Lisbon. He wants to book a flight next Friday.
5 Mr and Mrs Al-Omani have two children aged five and eight. They want to spend a week's holiday in Barcelona and can travel on a Monday or Tuesday.
6 Francis Ladd is going to Barcelona for a week but he wants to spend two days in Paris on his return journey. He can travel on any day of the week, if necessary.

7 Highway Holidays

A **Antigua** is the perfect choice for beach lovers. The people of the island are friendly and welcoming. The island itself is paradise on earth and the perfect place for sunbathing and simply doing nothing. Antigua does not offer a lot of exciting nightlife but most hotels have a little evening entertainment.

B A visit to **India** is a unique experience – an extra-ordinary mixture of races, religions and cultures. Each province or state in India is almost a world in itself, ranging from the peaceful lakes of Kashmir through the sun-baked deserts of Rajasthan and down to the beautiful beaches of Goa and the Arabian Sea. You'll compare the magnificent palaces of mighty Mohgul Emperors and world-famous monuments like the Taj Mahal with the busy city bazaars and the simple small villages.

C The Iguacu Falls are among the largest and most magnificent in the world. On this exciting holiday you will visit them by luxury coach, travelling on narrow roads through dense tropical forests all the way from Buenos Aires to Rio de Janeiro. On the way you will see wild animals, birds and insects of every kind. You will spend five nights in an international hotel in Puerto Iguazu, offering luxurious accommodation and superb food.

D Discover new tribes in *Papua New Guinea*. This adventure holiday will appeal to the young and energetic who are not easily frightened. But the rewards are great. They will be able to discover lost tribes and explore places never seen before by visitors.

E There's no place in the world like **Hong Kong**. Hong Kong boasts some of the finest shops in the world and you'll be able to buy many bargains there. Gold and jade jewellery, watches, cameras, computers, fashion-able clothes – all can be found in both big and small shops on any street.

F Visit **Rome**, the Eternal City. Look round the Forum and the Colosseum, and see the history of the Roman Empire. There are some of the world's finest museums and art galleries in Rome.

Which holidays would you recommend for the following people?

1 Abdul Khadum teaches history. He loves Italian food and is keen on art.
2 Anna Martinez and her husband feel that they need a rest. They want to have a very quiet holiday, relaxing on the beach.
3 Victor Kilimis is keen on wild life. He wants a holiday with lots of adventure but he doesn't like camping. He likes to sleep in a comfortable bed and eat good food on his holiday.
4 Mrs Ogasawara always wears smart clothes and loves spending her money on rings and bracelets. Her husband is keen on photography and wants to buy a new camera. He also wants to buy a very good computer but he cannot afford to spend too much on it.
5 Mr and Mrs Martin want to visit lots of interesting places and meet people of different races and cultures.
6 Antonio de Maria likes to do unusual things. Last year he sailed from Venice to Athens by himself in a small boat. He loves excitement.

UNIT ELEVEN

Sport

1 Look at the following football results for the League Cup. There is only one more match for Recife, Cabadelo ad Palmares to play. All the other teams have played all their matches this season.

	PLAYED	WON	DRAWN	LOST	POINTS
Recife	18	12	1	5	25
Olinda	19	8	8	3	24
Natal	19	10	1	8	21
Cabadelo	18	7	5	6	19
Nova Cruz	19	7	4	8	18
Caruaru	19	5	4	10	14
Palmares	18	3	3	12	9

Write out each number and the word which is missing. Use the information in the League Cup table.

Recife have already (1) _____ the League Cup. Although they have (2) _____ fewer matches than Olinda or Natal, they have (3) _____ more points. This season, Olinda have also had a very good (4) _____ . Although they have (5) _____ a lot of matches, not many teams have (6) _____ them. However, they have not (7) _____ as many matches as Natal, and Natal are third in the table. Cabdelo have (8) _____ both Nova Cruz and Caruaru in the League Table and they have (9) _____ 19 points from 18 matches. Palmares have been the least successful as they have (10) _____ 12 matches.

2 Work in pairs.

Read each of the following lists of five words. Guess the name of the sport or game to which the words belong.

1	net	2	court	3	rope
	serve		ball		hit
	ball		bounce		glove
	table		throw		ring
	bat		basket		referee

4	pitch	5	club	6	pedal
	referee		green		ride
	ball		course		saddle
	goal		drive		wheel
	kick		ball		handlebar

70

7	court	8	crawl	9	racquet
	ball		dive		net
	racquet		breaststroke		court
	serve		pool		smash
	net		float		shuttlecock

Now choose one of the sports or games from the lists and then write a few sentences describing it. Use the five words in the list.

3 Listen carefully to the talk about who will win a table tennis championship. As you listen, decide which player is most likely to win each match and play in the semi-finals. Then decide which two players will probably win the semi-finals and which player is likely to win the championship. Copy the table below and then write the names in it as you listen.

Dave Lynn
Ali Susie
Roger Mike
Steve Tina

4 Here are some sentences about tennis. Finish the second sentence so that it has the same meaning as the first.

1 Tennis is my favourite game.
Tennis is the game which I _____.
2 More people play tennis than badminton.
Not as _____.
3 No one is so old that he or she can't play tennis.
No one is too _____.
4 It isn't difficult to learn the rules of the game.
Learning _____.
5 You must hit the ball over the net.
It _____.

5 Listen to the tape recording and match each of the following names of sports and games with the appropriate sports report. Write the correct number after each letter in your exercise book.

A SWIMMING   B BOXING   C VOLLEYBALL   D TABLE TENNIS
E ATHLETICS   F CYCLING   G FOOTBALL   H HOCKEY

6 You will hear a recording of a radio programme about the sports events which are going to take place today. Write out these notes and complete them as you listen.

FOOTBALL

Place: (1) _____   Time: (2) _____
Hong Kong Under 21s v (3) _____ Under 21s.
Tickets: $20 – $40.   Reduction for (4) _____

BASKETBALL

Time: (5) _____   Place: Sekong Sports Centre
Yuen Long v Castle Peak
(Castle Peak = (6) _____ in Hong Kong League)

HOCKEY

Hong Kong Ladies v (7) _____
Place: Causeway Bay   Tickets: $20, $30.
Time: (8) _____
To be shown in TV programme called: (9) _____

SWIMMING

North Point Swimming Sports
Place: Thornton Baths   Tickets: (10) _____
Also water polo match. Suitable for (11) _____
Phone (12) _____ to book seats.

UNIT TWELVE

Jobs

1 There are six hidden words in the word square. The words are all in a straight line: some can be read forwards from left to right and others can be read downwards from top to bottom. You must never miss or jump letters. The six words are the names of jobs. When you have found them, match the right name with each of the sentences below the word square.

a	p	o	s	t	m	a	n	i	p	u
h	k	d	s	e	f	h	i	g	l	q
f	i	v	e	a	z	c	p	b	u	b
a	c	y	e	c	v	i	e	a	m	a
n	a	u	k	h	a	v	n	n	b	t
g	c	u	v	e	n	a	b	k	e	o
e	t	n	u	r	s	e	o	c	r	d
r	o	w	b	s	s	a	i	l	o	r
t	r	a	v	e	l	a	g	e	n	t
f	i	a	r	t	i	s	t	r	t	l

1   Anna Nascimento doesn't want to be a doctor or a teacher, but she likes taking care of sick children. She also likes looking after adults who are ill.
2   Nic Pavlidis is good at repairing things, especially water pipes, sinks and toilets.
3   Bill Cook is keen on travelling abroad and seeing different places. He wants to help his country and he is keen to learn new skills. He also likes to wear a uniform and look smart.
4   Amina Ismail wants to study at university. She is very keen on English and she is good at dealing with children.
5   Victor Lau wants an outdoor job which will give him plenty of exercise. He doesn't mind getting up early and he loves walking.
6   Anna Sillito wants an office job in her home town but she loves travelling, too. She has visited several foreign countries and is very good at getting information from timetables and arranging journeys.

2 Listen to the interview on the tape. If you agree with a statement, write YES after the number of the statement. If you do not agree, write NO.

1 Miss Chandra is applying for a job in a bookshop.
2 She has already had some experience of being a sales person in a publishing company.
3 The manager thinks she has good qualifications for the job.
4 Her reasons for applying for the job are rather poor.
5 The manager wants to find out if Miss Chandra can persuade people to do things.
6 Miss Chandra would show teachers all the books she had.
7 She would find out why teachers were not interested in certain books.
8 She seems to be keen and willing to work hard.

3 Work in pairs.

STUDENT A:
Copy out the following table into your exercise book.
1 Pretend to go for an interview for the first job. Student B will ask you questions about your ability to do a job as a **technician**. You must use the information in the table to answer the questions.
2 After answering the questions, you must then interview Student B. Ask questions to find out Student B's ability to do a job as a **nurse** and fill in the second line of the table.
3 Now change parts and let Student B ask you questions about your ability to do a job as a **reporter**. Work through the table in this way.

STUDENT B:
Turn to page 121. *Do NOT look at the following table.*

Student A's table

Job	Reason for applying	Ability to do the job	Attitudes	When able to start
Technician	Money	Fair	Likes tape recorders	Immediately
Nurse				
Reporter	Likes meeting people	Writes well	Prefers to write books	23 April
Clerk				
Soldier	Uniform	Strong; healthy	Loves adventure	In 3 months
Teacher				

4 Work in pairs.
Look at the list of jobs on the next page. Take it in turns to choose the three jobs which you think are best.

Discuss the reasons for your choice with your partner. Then choose the three jobs which you think are worst. Discuss your reasons again.

Policeman/Policewoman	Secretary	Engineer
Newspaper reporter	Doctor	Lawyer
Photographer	Pilot	Farmer
Computer scientist	Factory worker	Nurse
Accountant	Sales person	Air hostess
Lorry driver	Librarian	Pop singer
Electrician	Builder	Writer
Tourist guide	Teacher	Fashion designer

5 Look again at the list of jobs in the previous section. What was the job which you would most like to do? Write a short letter to a friend and tell him or her about the job. Write about:

i) the job
ii) the kind of work
iii) the hours
iv) the qualifications and training necessary for the job

v) any special ability needed
vi) your reasons for choosing the job
vii) the good things about the job
viii) the bad things about the job

6 Write out the following letter, putting in the words which are missing.

Dear Sir,
    I wish to apply for a (1) _____ as a tourist guide in the Transun Tourist Agency. I saw the (2) _____ in the Daily Times of 25th March.

    I am (3) _____ for the Preliminary English Test and I can speak a little English. I know the city and its surroundings well, and I am very (4) _____ in meeting people. History and geography were my favourite (5) _____ at school, and I can speak a little French in addition to my own language. My (6) _____ are photography and travel.

    I am sending you details about my education and the examinations which I have (7) _____ . References can be obtained from Mr G L Villar, Director of Studies, the British Council, and from Dr H T Sanchez, 61 Plaza de Colon. I am able to come for an (8) _____ at any time and I am free to start work at the beginning of next month.

    I very much look forward to (9) _____ from you.

                    (10) _____ faithfully,
                    Helena Latella

7   Look again at the letter in the previous section. Imagine that you have been successful in getting the job of tourist guide. Write a letter to a friend about your new job. Read the notes below and use them to describe your first day in the job. You should write about 80–100 words.

Showed group of 24 tourists round Buenos Aires – visited the Cathedral – tourists took lots of photographs – then went on visit to old harbour – next visited Ital Amusement Park – park crowded – lost two people in group – waited for half an hour – late for meal in restaurant at San Telmo – all tables full – had to wait – no time to take tourists shopping – everyone very tired, especially me!

8   Imagine that the following is your diary for next week showing some of your activities on certain days. First, fill in your activities for those days which have been left blank. Then use the information in your diary to write a letter to a friend. Tell him or her how you will spend your time. Write about 100 words. The address is not necessary.

1	MONDAY	Study!
2	TUESDAY	Final exams
3	WEDNESDAY	Shopping. Buy new clothes
4	THURSDAY	
5	FRIDAY	Interview
6	SATURDAY	
7	SUNDAY	Hope to start work tomorrow!

UNIT THIRTEEN

Hobbies

1 Look at this table and read the paragraph which follows it. Can you write the correct word after each number?

	Tracy	Haluk	Yusof	Silvia	Martina	Kenichi
Computer games			X			X
Rock music	X				X	
Swimming		X		X		X
Model making		X				
Photography					X	
Cycling				X	X	

(1) _____ hobby is listening to rock music. She also likes (2) _____ and (3) _____ . The other person who is keen on rock music is (4) _____ but this is her only hobby. (5) _____ is the other person in the group with only one hobby, but he likes (6) _____ . The most popular hobby is (7) _____ , but (8) _____ and (9) _____ are not as popular as the other hobbies listed in the table. (10) _____ seems to be very keen on sports as she likes both (11) _____ and (12) _____ . Kenichi has the same hobby as (13) _____ but he is also keen on swimming. (14) _____ , on the other hand, is keen on model making as well as (15) _____ .

2 Work in pairs. Look at the list of hobbies and pastimes on the next page. Which is your favourite hobby? Which hobby or pastime do you like the least? Discuss with your partner. Explain why you like or dislike these hobbies. Describe how often you do these activities and what you need to do them.

Next put all the hobbies in order, writing '1' against your favourite hobby, '2' against your second favourite hobby, '3' against your next, etc. When you have finished, discuss your list with your partner. You can also think of some other hobbies in which you are interested.

Going on picnics	Visiting museums	Photography
Dressmaking	Painting	Model making
Astronomy	Videos	Football
Basketball	Going to concerts	Table tennis
Science fiction	Pop music	Drama
Sightseeing	Playing the guitar	Computer games
Chess	Stamp collecting	Reading
Sailing	Fishing	Flying kites
Pets	Magic	Sewing
Knitting	Cooking	Dancing
Ice skating	Bird watching	Horse racing
Woodwork	Walking	Skiing

Which of the above pastimes usually take place
a) indoors   b) outdoors   c) both indoors and outdoors?

Which pastimes can be described as sports or games?

3   Listen carefully to the tape recording advertising a book club. Write the numbers of those sentences which you think are correct.

1 *Reading World* is a book club containing books about hobbies.
2 You must buy 20 books in order to join the club.
3 Write the titles of the books you want on a postcard.
4 When you first join, you will receive four books for $6.
5 The colour magazine contains the latest news about hobbies.
6 When you are a member, you must buy a book every two months.
7 You must write one month before you wish to leave the club.
8 When you join, you must promise not to leave the club.

4   Read the following description of a computer game called *Chinese Chess*.

In this excellent computer game you can play either against another player or against your computer. You use animals as chessmen and you must try to put one of your eight animals in the other player's den. You must also stop the other player from putting an animal in your den.

Each animal has its own place in the food chain, as shown in the table on the next page. An animal can eat any of the other animals below it. A dog can eat a cat and a mouse, a wolf can eat a dog, cat and mouse, and so on. However, elephant's cannot eat mice but mice can eat elephants.

All the animals can move one square left, right, up or down. Lions and tigers can jump over the water horizontally (to the left or right) but not vertically (up or down). Mice can swim in the water. None of the other animals can cross the water in any way at all.

Round the dens are three circles, called traps. An animal in a trap cannot be eaten, and so a way of guarding a den is to fill the traps with animals. Once in the traps, the animals themselves are safe from attack.

Animal	Order
Elephant	1
	2
Tiger	3
Leopard	4
	5
	6
Cat	7
	8

1 Copy out the table and write in it the names of the missing animals.
2 What can eat a tiger?
3 What can an elephant eat?
4 Which animals cannot jump over the water and cannot swim?
5 Why should you try to fill the traps with animals?
6 How can you win this game?

5 Work in pairs.

STUDENT A:

You are in a library and you want to borrow some books. Student B is the librarian and may ask you questions before suggesting some books to you. Read the sentences below and talk to the librarian.

1 You've just bought a camera and you're keen to use it.
2 You collect money from other countries but you don't save any paper money.
3 Your father likes growing flowers and vegetables.
4 You like swimming, but swimming from one side of a swimming pool to the other is very boring. You want to know what else you can do.
5 You love making and flying aeroplanes. Someone has just given you a radio so that you can control your planes in the air.
6 Your sister is keen on learning how to arrange flowers.

STUDENT B:

Turn to page 121.

6 Continue working in the same pairs.

STUDENT A:

Turn to pages 121 and 122.

STUDENT B:

You want to go on an activity holiday. You are 18 years old and very keen on driving. You are particularly interested in motor racing but you have never driven in a race and you know nothing about it. You would like to learn and to have a driving holiday for a week. Ask Student A about information on this kind of activity holiday: ask whether there are such holidays; ask how much they cost; and ask where they take place.

7 Read the following advertisement for a certain holiday.

ACTION HOLIDAYS
==
International Youth Centre, Almeria, Spain
==
Multi-activity holidays, April – October
for everyone aged 18 – 30
==

One-week holidays in beautiful countryside near Almeria. Learn new sports under expert instruction. Choose any THREE of the following activities for your week's course: flying, parachuting, ballooning, sailing, windsurfing, riding, climbing, skiing.

Accommodation in single rooms at a modern and well-equipped centre. TV, table tennis, small gymnasium and library. Only 36,000 pesetas a week including single room, all meals, all tuition and hire of equipment, etc.

Now imagine that you are just coming to the end of this holiday. It is your last day. You have kept a diary showing your activities on certain days. First, complete your activities for those days which have been left blank. (Choose a pastime which you like most.) Then use the information in your diary to write a letter to a friend. Tell him or her what you are doing on your holiday. Write about 100 words.

Begin your letter by writing the address of the youth centre in the top right-hand corner. Write today's date under it.

1	WEDNESDAY	Arrived at 4 p.m. Welcome party.
2	THURSDAY	Took first lesson in sailing.
3	FRIDAY	Climbed up cliff.
4	SATURDAY	
5	SUNDAY	Library in morning. Watched TV.
6	MONDAY	Climbed to top of Mount Alto.
7	TUESDAY	

8 Work in pairs.

STUDENT A:

Look at the photograph of two people sailing. Answer Student B's questions and talk to him or her about what you like/dislike doing.

STUDENT B:

Look at the photograph of two people sailing. Ask Student A the following questions and then talk to him or her about sailing and what you like/dislike doing.

Do you like sailing?

If Student A answers Yes, ask:

Where do you go sailing?

What do you enjoy most about it?

Is there anything you don't like about sailing?

If Student A answers No, ask:

What activities do you enjoy?

Which do you like best of all?

Why is it your favourite?

Is there anything you dislike about it?

9 Work in pairs.

Look at the photograph.

Now talk about the photograph and about yourself. These questions will help you.

Where do you think the boy in the photograph is?
What is the boy doing?
Do you enjoy playing board games?
What are your favourite games?
What are the indoor activities you enjoy most?
Why do you enjoy them?
What kind of games don't you like?
Why not?

UNIT FOURTEEN

Entertainment

1 Can they go there?

The following people want to do various things, but will they be able to? Read the newspaper notices which follow and write YES or NO after the number of each sentence below.

1 Mr Kilimis and his brother want to go to the theatre on Tuesday, 17 October to see *Macbeth*.
2 Susie Law would like to go to a disco but she has only £4.00.
3 Dave Archer would like to see the film *Dracula Returns* on Thursday evening, 19 October.
4 Mr and Mrs Sumito would like to listen to the London Symphony Orchestra on Saturday, 21 October.
5 Fatimah Aziz wants to listen to the New Festival Rock Group on Friday.
6 Carlos and Nina Santos want to watch two famous ice skaters at the Charlton City Rink on Sunday, 22 October.

A

New Festival Rock Group
Friday, 20 October
City Hall at 7.30 pm.
SOLD OUT

D

**EXHIBITION SKATING
BY
TORVILLE AND DEAN**
Sunday, 22 October
CANCELLED

B

London Symphony Orchestra
Friday, Saturday and Sunday
Tickets available only
for Friday and Saturday

E

CDE Cinema
Dracula Returns
11-18 October
Joe's Magic Dream
19-26 October

C

Shakespeare Festival
Hamlet: 12-14 October
Midsummer Night's Dream: 15 October
Macbeth: 16-19 October
Seats available for all nights

F

DISCO
New World Hall
9pm -1am
Tickets £2.50

2   Work in pairs.

STUDENT A:
   Turn to page 122.

STUDENT B:
   Student A works in the box office of a theatre. Book four seats at the theatre by telephone. You don't want to spend more than a total of £15 and you want to sit as near the front as possible but not at the end of a row.

Next Student A and Student B should change parts.

STUDENT A:
   Now Student B works in the box office of the theatre. Book seats for a party of 20 by telephone. You want good seats in the upper circle but you would like them to be as close together as possible.

STUDENT B:
   Turn to page 122.

3

Can you put the information about each programme with the most appropriate description which follows? Rewrite this extract from a TV programme guide, adding the correct description to each programme title.

5.00	**SPORTS**
6.00	**NEWS**
6.15	**CARTOON**
6.25	**DOCUMENTARY**
7.25	**COMEDY HALF-HOUR**
7.55	**QUIZ**
8.40	**VARIETY SHOW**
9.30	**DETECTIVE SERIAL**
10.30	**MORGAN'S CHAT SHOW**
11.00	**HORROR FILM**

1   Semi-finals. Today's special topic: Inventions and Discoveries.
    New Method College v King's School
2   Farming in Egypt – a look at some of the methods used today
3   Three Men on a Bicycle: more of the amusing adventures of Bill, Dave and Joe
4   Summary of today's events
5   The Queen's Singers, Mr Magic, the Rainbow Dancers, Al Cooley (a laugh a minute), and the New Moon Pop Group
6   World Cup: 4th round   Brazil v Spain
7   Part 3: The Missing Jewels
8   TV's most famous interviewer talks to more interesting guests
9   The Two-Headed Beast from the Bottom of the Sea
10 Mighty Mouse meets the Wicked Cat

EXAMPLE:
Sports
World Cup: 4th round   Brazil v Spain

4 First, copy out the boxes in your exercise books. Then listen to the tape recording giving information about three films. Write the correct letters in the boxes.

Write either
      LE (= The Last Emperor)
  or   M (= Mannequin)
  or WM (= White Mischief)

Note in Question 1:
    U = suitable for all ages
  PG = suitable for children if they see the film with their parents
  15 = no one under the age of 15 admitted
  18 = no one under the age of 18 admitted

1

U	
PG	
15	
18	

2

Historical	
Comedy	
Detective	
War	

3

England	
America	
Kenya	
China	

4

Excellent	
Good	
Fair	
Poor	

5 Here are some sentences about a certain film. Finish the second sentence so that it has the same meaning as the first.

1 There's a good film at the Odeon if you like detective films.
There's a good film at the Odeon for people _____ .

2 It's the best film we've seen this year.
We haven't seen _____ .

3 The film is so interesting that you won't want to miss a minute.
It's such _____ .

4 There is never a dull minute in the film.
Every minute _____ .

5 Steven Spielberg produced the film.
The film _____ .

6 The film has a lot of well-known stars in it.
There _____ .

7 It's advisable to book early if you want a good seat.
You _____ .

8 Unfortunately, no one under 18 is admitted.
Unfortunately, only those _____ .

6

CINEMAS: Manhattan, New York

WARNER CENTER, Park Avenue
Admission:
$15 adults; $10 children.
Screen 1   **Evil Beasts** 3.45, 6.00, 8.15
Screen 2   **Goodbye, Goodbye** 2.50, 5.20, 7.50
Screen 3   **La Bamba** 2.20, 4.55, 7.35
●
ROXY THEATER, Lexington Avenue
Admission:
$5 stalls; $7.50 circle. Children half price.
Star Trek 5.30, 8.00
●
CMN STUDIOS, E 53rd St
Admission:
Screen 1: $12.50; Screen 2: $9.00   No smoking.
Screen 1   **Top Gun** 3.20, 5.05, 8.40
Screen 2   **Evil Beasts** 2.30, 4.55, 7.20
●
CRESCENT MOVIE THEATER, Third Avenue
Admission:
$10 afternoons; $15 evenings after 5 pm
Screen 1   **Evil Beasts** 4.05, 6.10, 8.15
Screen 2   **Star Trek** 1.20, 5.05, 8.50
Screen 3   **Felix the Cat –**
              and other cartoons 2.30, 5.00

FILMS

● **Evil Beasts** Produced by Al Hitchin, master of suspense, this terrifying film will make your hair stand on end. You won't be able to sleep after seeing it!

● **Felix the Cat** This delightful cartoon will appeal to children of all ages. There are three other excellent cartoons in the same programme – good value for money.

● **Goodbye, Goodbye** A touching love story which will bring tears to your eyes, though parts of it tend to be rather slow. The haunting music perfectly matches the secret meetings and superb shots of the Californian countryside.

● **La Bamba** An Italian film about a small child who loses her parents. An old man looks after her and brings her up. A simple story, reminiscent of *Silas Marner* but set in Venice in 1988. (In Italian with English sub-titles.)

● **Star Trek 6** Yet another science fiction movie about Captain Kirk and his brave crew on board the Starship Enterprise, seeking out new stars and planets in the universe. In this film they visit the strangest planet of all only to discover that they are back on the Earth in 4000 AD.

● **Top Gun** A cowboy film which is different from most. An old gunfighter has hurt his hand and can no longer shoot as well as he could. He takes to the bottle and is happy at first to live on his memories. Then one day a notorious gang of bank robbers rides into town.

You are going to the cinema in New York and you want to check the information in the film guide which you are reading. Write the numbers of those statements which you think are correct.

1 There is a very good programme of cartoons showing on Screen 3 at the Crescent Movie Theater.
2 Children pay $5 less than adults at the Warner Center.
3 Three cinemas are showing a horror film.
4 All the films being shown at the Warner Center are in English.
5 The Roxy Theater in Lexington Avenue is showing a love story.
6 The cheapest cinema is the Crescent on Third Avenue.
7 A science fiction film is being shown at two of the cinemas.
8 Smoking is allowed in all the cinemas.
9 You can save $5 if you go to an afternoon performance at the Crescent Movie Theater.
10 The earliest performance starts on Screen 3 at the Warner Center.

7

● ● ● ● ● ● ● ●

THEATRE

● ● ● ● ● ● ● ●

● **Leeds Playhouse**
Calverley Street, Leeds. Tel. 442111
Restaurant and Bar
Oct 8–31 **Breaking the Silence** by
Stephen Poliakoff. Set in Russia in
1920, this is a powerful personal
drama and a vivid account of life at
that time.
Performances: Mon & Tues 8.00 pm
Wed – Sat 7.30 pm Sat mat. 3 pm
Admission: £3.50 – £6.
Student discounts available.

● **Civic Theatre**
Cookridge Street, Leeds.
Tel. 455505/462453
Drinks and snacks available.

Oct 7–10 **California Suite** by Neil
Simon. Hotel comedy performed by
the Leeds Art Theatre Company.
Performances: 7.30 pm.
Admission: £2.

Oct 13–17 Leeds Art Centre
presents **As You Like It** by
William Shakespeare.
Performances: 7.30 pm.
Admission: £3.

Oct 21–24 Proscenium Players
present **Pack of Lies** by Hugh
Whitemore, a spy drama.

Performances: 7.30 pm.
Admission: £2.

● **Grand Theatre**
New Briggate, Leeds.
Tel. 459351/440971
Oct 19–24 Leeds Operatic Society
present **Can-Can**. Be taken back in
time to Paris in 1880 with the
unforgettable music of Cole Porter.
Performances: 7.15 pm nightly.
Sat Matinee 2 pm
Admission: £5.50–£1.50; 20p per
person off parties of 10 or more

● **Alhambra**
Prince's Way, Bradford. Tel. 752000
Bar and Restaurant
Week beginning October 5.
Victoria Wood. One of TV's funniest
women takes a sharp look at life.
Performances: 7.30 pm.
Admission: £8.50–£5.

● **City Varieties**
The Headrow, Leeds. Tel. 430808
Oct 10 & 11 only **A Night at the
Varieties** All the fun of an old music
hall with Barry Cryer, Duggie
Brown, 6 dancers, Mystina, Jon
Barker, Anne Duval and the Tony
Harrison Trio. Laugh again at the
old jokes and listen to your
favourite songs.
Performances: 8 pm nightly
Admission: £5.50; under 16 or
over 60 £4.

● **York Theatre Royal**
St Leonard's Place, York. Tel. 23568

Sep 23–Oct 17 **Groping for Words** –
a comedy by Sue Townsend. Best
known for her Adrian Mole Diaries,
Townsend now writes about an
evening class which two men and a
woman attend. A gentle comedy.
Admission: First night, Mon and
matinees: £2.50; Tues–Fri:
£3.25–£5.50; Sat £3.50–£5.75.

● **Halifax Playhouse**
King's Cross Street, Halifax.
Tel. 65998
Oct 10–17 **On Golden Pond** by
Ernest Thompson. This is a magical
comedy about real people. A
beautifully produced, well-acted
play for everyone. Don't miss it.
Performances: 7.30.
Admission: £2. Mon: 2 seats for
the price of one.

● **Harrogate Theatre**
Oxford Street, Harrogate.
Tel. 502116. Bar and Buffet.
Oct 1–17 **The Secret Diary of
Adrian Mole, aged 13½** .
Sue Townsend's musical play,
based on her best-selling book.
Performances: Evenings 7.45.
Matinees on October 10 & 17, at
2.30. No Monday performances.
Admission: Tues–Thurs: £2–£5.
Fri & Sat: £2–£6.

You are going to give some people information about local theatres in Leeds, Bradford, York, Halifax and Harrogate. Before you start, check the notes below, using the Theatre Guide taken from an information guidebook called 'Where and When'. Put a tick (√) after the number of each note which is correct. Put a cross (×) after the number of each note which is incorrect.

1 On October 14 you can see a play by Shakespeare at the Civic Theatre in Leeds.
2 The cheapest seats at two of the theatres are less than £2 each.
3 The same person has written two of the plays in the Guide.
4 You can get something to drink and eat at three of the theatres in the list.
5 One of the theatres is closed on Monday evenings.
6 If you want to see a musical, ring 75200 to book a seat.
7 Seats for the play *On Golden Pond* will cost only £1 each on a Monday night if two people go.
8 Three similar kinds of plays are being performed at Leeds Civic Theatre.
9 The person who is performing at the Alhambra Theatre in Bradford is a television star.
10 The person who wrote this information in the Theatre Guide did not like the play being performed in Halifax.
11 Leeds Operatic Society is performing at the Civic Theatre on October 22.
12 There are at least three comedies being performed on the evening of October 10.

UNIT FIFTEEN

Countries

1 Work in pairs.

STUDENT A:

Turn to page 122 and look carefully at Map A1. Student B is going on holiday to Teneroga and will ask you questions about the map. Tell Student B where the different places are. Describe the map but take care not to show the map to Student B.

STUDENT B:

Look at Map B1 below and try to complete it. Student A will tell you where the various places are on the map. Try to complete the map from the information given. You can ask questions but you must not look at Student A's map.

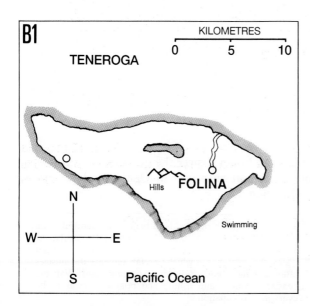

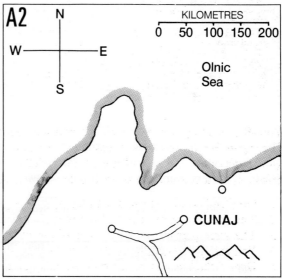

Students A and B should now do the same with Maps A2 and B2.

STUDENT A:

Look at Map A2 and complete the map from the information given.

STUDENT B:

Turn to page 123 and describe Map B2 to Student A.

2 Write out the following notes and complete them as you listen to the short talk about Portugal.

PORTUGAL

Position: _____

Size (compared with Ireland): _____

Area: _____

Rivers: (1) _____

       (2) _____

       (3) _____

Climate: _____

Average temperature: _____ Highest temperature: _____

Capital: _____

Population: _____

Language: _____

3 Write sentences like the one in the example. Use words which show nationalities (eg *the English*) in place of the names of countries (eg *England*).

Example: A lot of tea is drunk in England.

The English drink a lot of tea.

1 A lot of rice is grown in China.
2 The best cameras are made in Japan.
3 A lot of football is played in Brazil.
4 Kilts are worn in Scotland.
5 Beautiful carpets are made in Turkey.
6 Some good cheese is made in Holland.
7 French, German and Italian are spoken in Switzerland.
8 A lot of potatoes are eaten in Britain each year.

4 Read the following information about New Zealand and then answer the questions which follow. You must write out the letter (A, B, C or D) of the correct answer(s) in Questions 1, 2 and 8. (**Note: There is more than one correct answer for Question 2.**)

It is not unusual for Auckland to be compared to Sydney or San Francisco. Visually they do have much in common. All three hillside cities are built around a beautiful harbour, each with its own bridge linking the northern and southern sides. However, most Aucklanders would agree that it would be presumptuous to carry the comparison further for Auckland is Auckland, a city with a character much different from Sydney or San Francisco.

Built on seven hills (actually seven extinct volcanoes), Auckland is in area one of the largest cities in the world although its population is barely one million. In the early days of European settlement, Auckland was New Zealand's capital, but this was transferred to the more centrally situated Wellington before the turn of the century, a fact which Aucklanders still consider unreasonable.

Thirty miles north of Auckland begin the beautiful small inlets and harbours of the Whangaparoa Peninsula. At Waiwera you will find hot springs just like fountains of hot water, the ideal spot in which to relax and ease the muscles after a long flight. Between Auckland and Waiwera beaches abound, and fishing and boating appear to be everyone's occupation.

Within the environs of Auckland itself, however, are some excellent beaches, especially at Takapuna on the northern side of the bridge and also at Orakei and St Heliers on the southern side. It is certainly worth a drive around the scenic route of the harbour. On the west coast at places like Piha there are black sand beaches where the Tasman Sea rolls in waves which are a surfer's dream.

1 This is from
    A a novel.
    B a geography textbook.
    C a letter.
    D a tourist guidebook.

2 Auckland, Sydney and San Francisco all have
    A hills.
    B bridges.
    C beautiful harbours.
    D similar characters.

3 Although only one million people live in Auckland, it _____ .

4 Wellington became the capital of New Zealand instead of Auckland because _____ .

5 What did the people of Auckland think about this change?

6 How can you relax in Waiwera?

7 What are two popular activities?

8 Which sport is Piha good for?
    A Fishing
    B Boating
    C Surfing
    D Diving

5 Write answers to the following questions.

1 Where do you live?
2 How many people live there?
3 Is it in the north, in the west, etc?
4 What do you think a visitor would like to see?
5 What is there to do?

Now use your answers to write a short letter to a penfriend. Tell your penfriend about the place where you live.

6 Listen to these six short conversations. If you agree with a sentence below about a conversation, write YES. If you do not agree, write NO.

1 The woman disagrees with the man about Australia.
2 The man is correcting the woman.
3 The man is complaining about the country he visited.
4 The woman is apologising to the man about the lack of good hotels and restaurants.
5 The woman is happy about moving to the south.
6 The man and the woman are arguing about shopping.

7 Listen to the conversation on the tape. Write the numbers of those statements which you think are correct.

1 The woman thinks Brasilia isn't different in any way from all other modern cities.
2 The man likes the tall blocks of flats in Brasilia.
3 The woman thinks that Brasilia is rather dirty.
4 The woman complains about the lack of culture in Brasilia.
5 'Instant Brazil' is the name of a tour to several countries near Brasilia.
6 The woman thinks it takes a long time to learn about the culture of another country.
7 The man says that Brasilia has a large, well-planned airport.
8 The woman has just visited Brasilia.

UNIT SIXTEEN

Food and Restaurants

1 Read the following notice.

YOUR GUIDE TO GOOD HEALTH

Eat well and enjoy life

- Eat less butter. ● Eat more fish. ● Eat more vegetables and far less meat. ● Eat salads rather than pies. ● Cut down on sugar and eat fruit instead of cakes and puddings. ● Say NO to fatty or fried food.

Now put the following items of food into two categories: HEALTHY FOOD and UNHEALTHY FOOD. (Use a dictionary if necessary.)

spinach	cabbage	apples	chocolate
bananas	hamburgers	sausages	lettuce
pork pies	fried fish	butter	steamed fish

Discuss your answers in small groups.

2 Work in pairs.

Activity 1

STUDENT A:

You are a customer in a small restaurant. Look carefully at the menu below and ask the waiter (Student B) for advice about various dishes. You are a vegetarian and your favourite vegetables are mushrooms. Unfortunately, you cannot stand cheese of any kind but, on the other hand, you eat fish occasionally. Although you love salads, on this occasion you would prefer something hot to eat.

To start	Main Course	To finish
Soup of the day	Chef's speciality	Sherry trifle
Cocktail à la maison	Swiss fondue	Chef's special pudding
Home-made paté	Risotto Milanese	Black Forest Gateaux
Parma ham and melon	Lamb à la maison	Cheese (and biscuits)
	Shepherd's pie	
	Lobster salad	
	Grilled Dover sole	Coffee, tea

STUDENT B:

Turn to page 123.

Activity 2

STUDENT A:

Turn to page 123.

STUDENT B:

You are now a customer in a small restaurant. Look carefully at the menu on the previous page and ask the waiter (this time Student A) for advice on ordering various dishes. You like spicy food very much but you also like to try out the local dishes of the country which you are visiting. You cannot eat pork, food cooked in wine or shell fish of any kind.

3 Listen to the conversation on the tape. Write the numbers of those sentences which you think are correct.

1   The man disagrees with the woman about Chinese food in Bangkok.
2   He thinks the Chinese food in Hong Kong is better than that in Bangkok.
3   The woman has never been to any Chinese restaurants in Hong Kong.
4   Both the man and woman agree about Chinese restaurants in Europe.
5   The man thinks that the vegetables are not cooked long enough in most restaurants in Bangkok.
6   The man agrees with the woman that there are a lot of different kinds of Chinese food in Bangkok.
7   The man thinks there is too much chilli in all the Chinese food in Bangkok restaurants.
8   He doesn't think there is even one good restaurant in Bangkok.
9   The woman thinks the Canton restaurant is one of the best in the world.
10   The man never gives any reasons for his low opinion of Chinese restaurants in Bangkok.

4 Here are some sentences about food and restaurants. Finish the second sentence so that it has the same meaning as the first.

1   It isn't necessary to sit exactly in the Japanese way when you eat.
You _____ .
2   However, you won't be able to sit on chairs at a table.
However, it won't _____ .
3   It will still be necessary to sit on the straw mat floor.
You will still _____ .
4   Almost all the dishes are eaten with chopsticks.
People use _____ .
5   Most foreigners dislike sashimi at first even though it is very popular with the Japanese.
Most foreigners dislike sashimi at first in spite _____ .
6   We recommend maki-zushi for foreigners who are trying Japanese food for the first time.
Maki-zushi _____ .

5   Read the following extracts. Can you put each extract with the correct heading?

1   NEWSPAPER REVIEW   2   ADVERTISEMENT   3   NOVEL
4   FOOD AND HEALTH BOOK   5   RECIPE   6   LETTER

A   The amount of food required by the average adult depends on the kind of work which he or she is doing. A person working behind a desk for much of the time will need less than someone doing heavy physical work.

B   Mr Yakimoso and I had a marvellous dinner yesterday evening. After we'd met a few people from the office, we all went to the Shangrila Restaurant in Yokohama – an excellent restaurant serving first-class Chinese food. Do you know it at all? The next time you come to Yokohama, I must take you there.

C   Heat the oil in a very hot pan and put in 3 ozs of mungbean sprouts. When hot, stir and pour in the prepared stock and black mushrooms. Bring to the boil, adding crab meat and thickening the sauce with cornflour. Add sesame oil to taste, sprinkle with white leek and pour over the noodles.

D   *Ringo's* boasts of its atmosphere and its superb Italian cooking. The candlelit tables and the small orchestra certainly help the restaurant to live up to its first claim. Although some of the dishes were only average, most of the main courses were of a very high standard. In particular, the saltimbocca was excellent. It was served on a bed of white rice and served with spinach and courgettes.

E   Several people were leaving as Gerry and Dianne approached Maxim's. 'Good, we may be able to get our favourite table near the window,' Dianne whispered.
'It's a pity Harry forgot to book a table for us,' sighed Gerry.
As soon as they entered the small dimly-lit restaurant, the head waiter came up to them, bowed and snapped his fingers at another waiter.

F   SILVIO'S 25 Shaw Lane, Headington, Bristol
For the very best Italian food
Taste our magical minestrone, mouth — watering pizzas, delicious spaghetti dishes and fantastic desserts. We are certain that you'll come back for more!
OPEN 12 — 3 and 6 — 11.30 Tuesdays to Saturdays Tel 544396

6   Now answer these further questions about some of the extracts.

1   What is the writer trying to do in extract A?
    A   To be amusing and entertain.
    B   To give information and advice.
    C   To frighten and shock people.
    D   To give a description.
2   What does the writer think that the best dish is in extract D?
3   Why did the head waiter snap his fingers in extract E?
4   In extract F why does the writer think that people will want to return to the restaurant?

7

Restaurant Attica	Our greatest asset is the Patron, Dimitris,	Bridgegate
Greek Specialities	who welcomes you personally.	Sydney
Kebabs · Moussaka · Meza	Here you can relax with a drink or coffee after your meal.	*Tel. 492877*
Steaks · Roasts · Pasta	Excellent food, friendly service, and comfortable and attractive surroundings.	

You saw this advertisement in last Saturday's newspaper. You decided to visit the restaurant with three friends. The food was not too expensive but the wine was very dear indeed. You all enjoyed your meal apart from the vegetables (which were cold). Unfortunately, you had to wait almost 40 minutes before you were served.

The manager of the restaurant has given you a questionnaire. He has asked you to fill it in truthfully. Give details about yourself in the first part of the form and then use the information above to complete the second part of the form. Write out the form and your answers in your exercise books.

QUESTIONNAIRE: Did you like our restaurant?

Full name: _____ Mr/Mrs/Miss/Ms
Address: _____

_____

Your favourite dish: _____
Kind of food you like (eg English, French, Chinese, etc): _____

_____

Number of people in your party: _____
How you knew about this restaurant: _____
Any comments on:–
(1) the food _____
(2) the service _____
(3) the cost _____
Would you recommend this restaurant to your friend? _____
Reasons: _____
Suggest how it could be improved: _____

Any other comments: _____

_____

Signature: _____ Date: _____

8 Read the following passage and then answer the questions which follow. You must choose the correct answer or write a few words.

Eating at the new CANTON ALACARTE restaurant is an experience you will not forget – that is, if you're lucky enough to be served. When I went with a small party of friends, we waited almost one hour before we were even given a menu. Although the waiters are always polite, friendly and apologetic, the adjective *slow* is an under-statement.

Fortunately, the restaurant is very attractive inside and a leisurely drink at the comfortable bar is not at all un-pleasant. A waiter is always ready to fill up your glass but strangely enough not very willing to show you to your table.

When you take your seat at your table and the first dish eventually arrives, it looks delicious. The cold dish we had as a starter brought gasps of admiration from all around when it was served. But the food itself had no flavour at all. The other courses – chicken and walnuts, beef and bamboo shoots, pork dumplings – were just as tasteless. The only thing that was worthy of note was the bill – £168 for 6. Perhaps I had now better get a job helping the chef!

1 This is from
   A an advertisement.
   B a newspaper.
   C a letter.
   D a novel.

2 What is the writer trying to do?
   A To persuade people to go to the restaurant.
   B To give a detailed description of the restaurant.
   C To warn people about the restaurant in an amusing way.
   D To give as much information as possible.

3 The writer thinks that the chief weakness of the food is that _____

4 What does he say about the service in the restaurant?

5 In the writer's opinion, the staff of the restaurant want people
   A to spend money on drinking.
   B to relax before they eat.
   C to eat the food quickly.
   D to offer to help in the kitchen.

9 Imagine that your rich uncle took you to the *Canton Alacarte* restaurant. However, you had a very good meal there, and the service was fast and efficient. Write a letter to a friend of yours, telling him/her about your visit to the restaurant and saying how much you enjoyed the meal there.

READING

Question 1 Look at the five pictures of signs below.

Someone asks you what each sign means. For each sign put a tick in one of the boxes to show the correct answer.

1.

LIBRARY
SILENCE

☐ The library is closed.

☐ You cannot smoke in the library.

☐ No talking in the library.

☐ The library doesn't have records.

2.

BARGAINS
all prices reduced

☐ There are fewer bargains now.

☐ Prices are lower than before.

☐ Fewer goods are now on sale.

☐ Everything has already been sold.

3.

OFFICE HOURS
Mon–Fri: 8am–6pm
Sat: 8am–1pm
*This office is open to visitors
at the times stated above.*

☐ The office is open every morning apart from Sunday.

☐ The office is open all day at the weekend.

☐ The office is open every afternoon from Monday to Saturday.

☐ The office is open only three days every week.

4.

NEWTOWN COLLEGE
—
Only teachers
beyond this point

☐ Students should walk past this notice.

☐ Only teachers can go any further.

☐ Only teachers should wait here.

☐ Students should meet their teacher at this place.

5.

● **Book before 31 March**

AND SAVE £50

on your holiday

☐ If you save £50 before 31 March, you can book a holiday.

☐ You can book a holiday before 31 March if you pay £50 now.

☐ You must book before 31 March if you want a holiday for £50.

☐ If you book before 31 March, your holiday will cost you £50 less.

Question 2 Read the paragraph below. It is the story of a holiday in Italy. Circle the letter next to the word that best fits each space.

EXAMPLE:

I'd like to .... you about my holiday in Italy.

A. say   B. speak   Ⓒ tell   D. talk

    Recently we went on (1) .... to Italy. We (2) .... a flight from London to Naples and then took a bus to Sorrento.

    The (3) .... from the airport to Sorrento took over an hour and we were very tired (4) .... we arrived at the hotel. (5) .... our room was on the seventh (6) .... , we had a lovely (7) .... overlooking the bay. Sorrento was full of (8) .... , but it was still very nice. We went on a coach to see the ruins of Pompey and we also took a (9) .... to the Isle of Capri. Everything was so enjoyable until we returned to London and found some of our (10) .... missing. They had put it on the wrong plane!

---

(1)	A holiday	B the holiday	C holidays	D some holidays
(2)	A bought	B left	C booked	D kept
(3)	A way	B journey	C travel	D distance
(4)	A since	B when	C for	D while
(5)	A For	B Since	C Although	D Where
(6)	A floor	B level	C number	D ground
(7)	A scene	B sight	C look	D view
(8)	A travellers	B passers-by	C tourists	D spectators
(9)	A trip	B way	C travel	D journey
(10)	A container	B bag	C luggage	D contents

Question 3 Below are some pictures of medicine on sale in a chemist's shop. Read the labels on these bottles, jars and packets. Then decide which are suitable for each of the persons described.

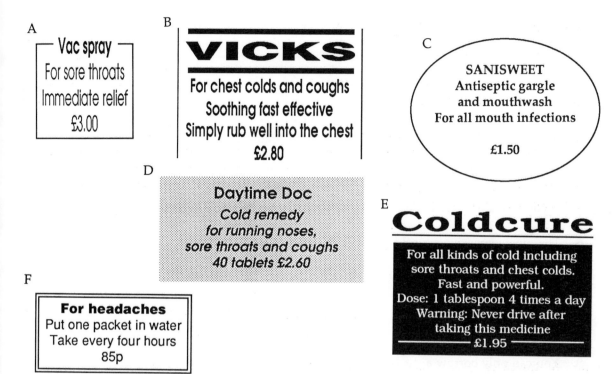

A
Vac spray
For sore throats
Immediate relief
£3.00

B
VICKS
For chest colds and coughs
Soothing fast effective
Simply rub well into the chest
£2.80

C
SANISWEET
Antiseptic gargle
and mouthwash
For all mouth infections
£1.50

D
Daytime Doc
Cold remedy
for running noses,
sore throats and coughs
40 tablets £2.60

E
Coldcure
For all kinds of cold including
sore throats and chest colds.
Fast and powerful.
Dose: 1 tablespoon 4 times a day
Warning: Never drive after
taking this medicine
£1.95

F
For headaches
Put one packet in water
Take every four hours
85p

Which medicine is suitable for the following people? Put a tick in the boxes for every kind of medicine that is suitable for each person. Note that more than one medicine is suitable for some of the people.

	A	B	C	D	E	F
Mr Sampson has just caught a bad cold and has to blow his nose every few minutes.						
Mrs Lee has a small ulcer on her tongue. It is rather sore.						
Miss Henley has a bad cold and sore throat but must drive a long way to her sister's house.						
Mr Browning has a nose cold but he doesn't want to carry bottles of medicine with him.						
Miss Pawley has a sore throat but she doesn't want to spend more than £2 on medicine.						
Mr Neilson has just recovered from a bad cold but he now has a headache.						
Mr Wright's throat is sore only because he has sung all day. He wants to sing again very soon.						
Mrs Hall doesn't like taking medicine for her bad cough but she doesn't mind rubbing ointment on her skin.						

Question 4 A friend of yours is thinking of either buying or borrowing a car to use on a long visit to Britain. Look at the advertisements below and on page 101. If you think the statements below are correct, put a tick in the box under YES. If you think they are not correct, put a tick in the box under NO.

		YES	NO
1.	Nu-Reg Autos charge less than the ordinary price for their cars.	☐	☐
2.	Stuart Gater sells Honda cars.	☐	☐
3.	West Yorks Motor Group sell Fiat cars in both Bradford and Keighley.	☐	☐
4.	You can borrow any make of car if you phone 0384 442266.	☐	☐
5.	If you buy a new car at Seftons, it will probably be delivered to you at once.	☐	☐
6.	The most expensive car sold by Nu-Reg Autos is the Maestro 1.6 Mayfair.	☐	☐
7.	Vincents of Reading sell only new cars.	☐	☐
8.	If you want to buy a car without paying tax, you should phone Kestrel Export Cars.	☐	☐
9.	You can only borrow a car from First National Contracts for one, two or three years.	☐	☐
10.	National Finance and Leasing will buy your old car if you buy a new car from them.	☐	☐

SEFTONS

HONDA SPECIALISTS IN WEST MIDLANDS
DOWNTON ROAD, EXHALL, COVENTRY
TEL: (0203) 729200
Immediate delivery on most models
Also a selection of quality used Hondas available
Leasing demonstrations and good delivery

TAX-FREE CARS
LHD–RHD
Special Deals on Mercedes
Tel: 010 32 59 32 1314
KESTREL EXPORT CARS
Yzerlaan 3, 8401 Bredene
Near Ostend, Belgium
Telex: 81762 KEST B (38282)

Vincents
for used BMW

VINCENTS
OF READING

209-211 Shinfield Road,
Reading, Berks.
Tel: (0734) 866161

*Just 5 minutes from
M4 Junction 11*   *Approved Used Cars*
33705

Question 5 Read the passage and then answer the questions which follow. You must put a tick in the correct box or write in a few words.

Mr Selwyn Hanson has worked as a clerk for this company for almost one year. Previously, he was employed for six months by Dingle, Hall and Company as a junior clerk and then for four months in a similar job by Smith and Wright Limited. His typing speed is slightly below average, and he could be more accurate. However, he has improved a little during his time in the company.

Mr Hanson is always cheerful and is a very popular member of our staff. His fondness for practical jokes is sometimes a little difficult to understand but his intentions are generally good. He is conscientious on the whole and works fairly hard most of the time until he loses his ability to concentrate. He is usually punctual but has been absent on several occasions as a result of minor illnesses. He is extremely loyal to the firm and is always most willing to do many small jobs which are not normally his responsibility.

Mr Hanson has just started to learn how to use an Apple Word Processor. He has a home computer and he has developed a confidence in using computers and word processors. Confidence is a quality which Mr Hanson does not lack: sometimes, in fact, Mr Hanson's ability does not justify such a high degree of confidence.

I feel that Mr Hanson could be reasonably successful as an assistant stores officer in your company provided that he is well supervised and not too much is expected of him.

---

1. This is from   ☐   a letter.

                   ☐   a book.

                   ☐   an advertisement.

                   ☐   a magazine.

2. What is the writer really   ☐   His worry about Mr Hanson's health.
   expressing?

                   ☐   A little praise and a lot of criticism of Mr Hanson.

                   ☐   Admiration for Mr Hanson's unusual qualities.

                   ☐   Neither praise nor criticism of Mr Hanson.

3. The writer says that Mr Hanson cannot type ....

4. What particular qualities in Mr Hanson does the writer like most of all?
   ....

5. What is the writer saying about Mr Hanson?

     ☐   The writer is recommending Mr Hanson extremely highly and ignores his faults.

     ☐   The writer is recommending Mr Hanson quite highly and thinks his faults are unimportant.

☐ The writer is not recommending Mr Hanson too highly and draws attention to his faults.

☐ The writer is not recommending Mr Hanson at all and ignores his qualities.

WRITING

Question 6 Here are some sentences about sports and games. Finish the second sentence so that it has the same meaning as the first.

EXAMPLE:

Italy won their match against Spain.

Spain *lost their match against Italy.* ....

1. Bangkok has some excellent sports grounds.
   There ....

2. In the new sports centre you can play tennis even in winter.
   In the new sports centre it ....
   ....

3. In Japan people now play baseball in both winter and summer.
   In Japan baseball ....
   ....

4. Tennis matches are often stopped in England because it rains heavily.
   Tennis matches are often stopped in England because of ....
   ....

5. In Australia swimming is more popular than cycling.
   In Australia cycling isn't ....

Question 7 You are applying for a scholarship to go on a three-month study tour of any country you want to visit. Fill in the application form below giving details about yourself.

APPLICATION FOR STUDY TOUR

Surname: .... Mr/Mrs/Miss Other names ....

Nationality: .... Age on Jan 1 this year .... years .... months

Home address: ....

....

....

College/University (Give year): ....

Examinations passed: ....

Prizes won (for your studies/work/sports, etc): ....

Subject you wish to study: ....

Reason for choice of subject: ....

Country you wish to visit: ....

Reason for choice of country: ....

....

If not possible, state what other country you wish to visit: ....

Hobbies: ....

Write a sentence saying why you think you deserve a scholarship for a study tour.

....

....

How do you think the study tour will help you in your future career?

....

....

Signature .... Date ....

Question 8 Imagine that this was the tour programme for a holiday you planned last year. You have now been on the holiday. Fill in Day 6 and then use the information in the tour programme to write a letter to a friend about how you spent your time. Write about 100 words. The address is not necessary.

1	DAY 1	Fly to Morocco; coach from airport to Agadir
2	DAY 2	Morning: relax in hotel Afternoon: beach
3	DAY 3	Coach trip to Atlas Mountains
4	DAY 4	Shopping
5	DAY 5	Day: Fishing Evening: Folk Concert
6	DAY 6	
7	DAY 7	Return to London

....

....

....

....

....

....

....

....

LISTENING

Question 9 Put a tick in the box you think is the most suitable.

EXAMPLE:

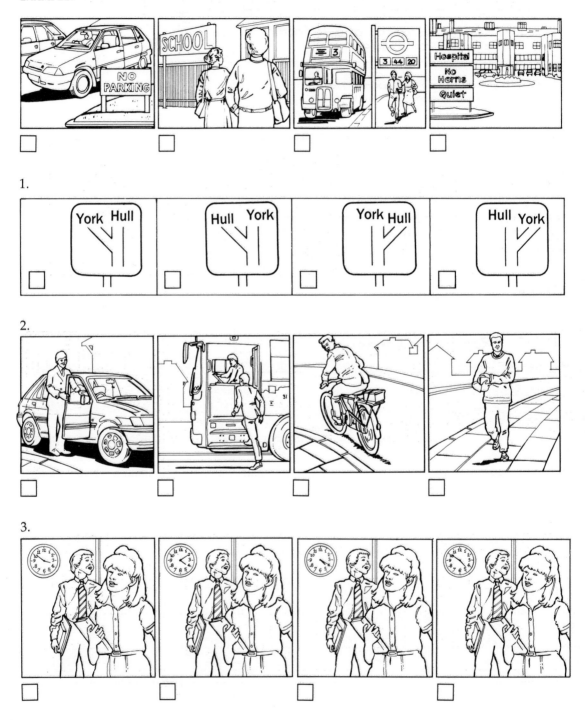

1.

2.

3.

4.

5.

6.

7.

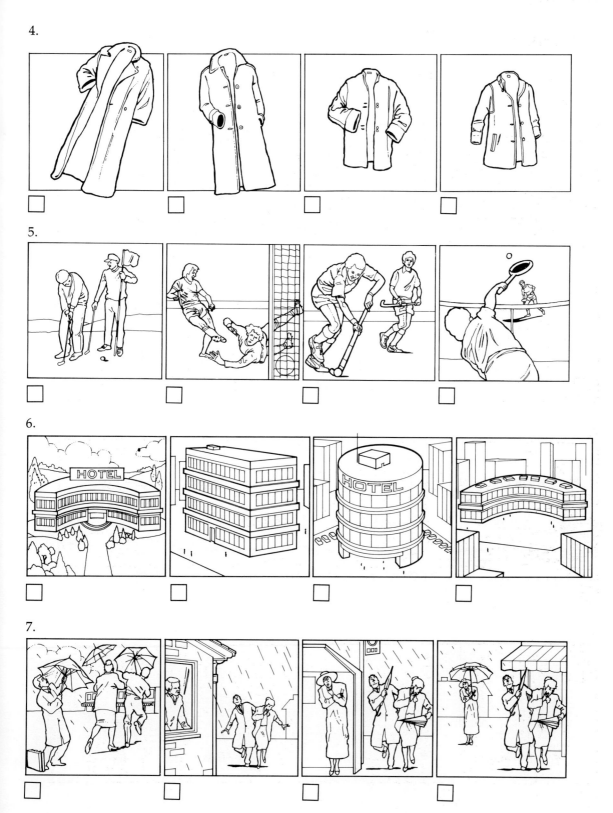

Question 10 Listen to the weather report and put a tick in the boxes you think are the most suitable.

1. Weather in Britain

   – similar to that in:

   France ☐

   Germany ☐

   Sweden ☐

   Denmark ☐

2. Monday in Britain:

   snow ☐

   rain ☐

   sunshine ☐

   fog ☐

3. Sunday in Ireland:

   very wet all the time ☐

   cloudy at times ☐

   very cold all the time ☐

   sunny at times ☐

4. Temperature:

   13° C ☐

   15° C ☐

   20° C ☐

   30° C ☐

5. Wednesday evening:

   frost ☐

   fog ☐

   snow ☐

   sunshine ☐

6. Sunshine and clear skies at the weekend over:

   northern England ☐

   central England ☐

   southern England ☐

   Scotland ☐

Question 11 A friend of yours wants some advice about restaurants in Harrogate. Fill in the information needed below and tick the boxes you think are the most suitable.

DA MARIO'S

English ☐   Italian ☐   French ☐   Indian ☐

Recommended dish: ....

Dessert: ....

Price = ...

Price includes:–

soup ☐   main dish ☐   dessert ☐   coffee ☐   wine ☐

THE SHABAB

Italian ☐   Indian ☐   French ☐   Pakistani ☐

Recommended dish: ....

Other dishes: ....

Price = ...

Price includes:–

soup ☐   main dish ☐   dessert ☐   coffee ☐   wine ☐

Question 12 If you agree with the statement, put a tick in the box under YES. If you do not agree, put a tick in the box under NO.

		YES	NO
1.	*EastEnders* is about some ordinary people in London.	☐	☐
2.	The woman is keen on *EastEnders*.	☐	☐
3.	She thinks that the Beales' flat looked very attractive.	☐	☐
4.	The man has become very interested in the daily lives of the characters in *EastEnders*.	☐	☐
5.	The detective film is called *The Wolf's Tongue*.	☐	☐
6.	Both the man and the woman agree that the Inspector Morse film will be very good.	☐	☐
7.	*It'll Be Alright On The Night* will follow the detective film.	☐	☐
8.	*It'll Be Alright On The Night* is a programme about memory and forgetting things.	☐	☐
9.	Both the man and the woman like *It'll Be Alright On The Night*.	☐	☐
10.	Both the man and the woman are going to stay at home in order to watch television.	☐	☐

SPEAKING

For this part of the examination, work in pairs.

Section I

First, give each other your names and spell them. Then ask questions about each other: ask about each other's ages, families, brothers and sisters, their ages, father's occupation, etc.

Section II

One student should take the part of Student A and the other the part of Student B.

Student A:
  Turn to page 123.
Student B:
  Listen to Student A. He/She will ask you to go to an exhibition. You would like to go very much, but you are very busy during this period. It will obviously be quite difficult to arrange a suitable day and time to go. Nevertheless, try your best to arrange to go with Student A.

Section III

One student should look at Photograph A on the third page of the colour section in the centre of the book. The other student should look at Photograph B on the fourth page of the colour section.

You should not see each other's photograph at first when you describe your photograph. You should talk freely about your own photograph and ask questions about your partner's photograph. In this way, you and your partner should discover the similarities and differences through your descriptions. In the later stages of the discussion, you may see each other's photograph.

Section IV

The men in the two pictures you've just described are busy at work in a house. Now find out what kind of jobs your partner likes doing or doesn't like doing in his/her house or flat.

TECHNIQUES

The following pages give information about the types of questions in the Preliminary English Test, together with some advice about answering these questions. The figures in the boxes refer to the numbers of the exercises and test items contained in this book. Note that many other exercises and activities in this book also give useful practice in answering questions in the Preliminary English Test. Only those exercises which are exactly *identical* in form, however, are given in the boxes here.

Note the meaning of the abbreviations and numbers in the boxes: eg

> PT1 = Practice Test 1: Question 1
> 2.7 = Unit 2: Section 7

READING

‖ QUESTION 1 ‖

In this question you will see photographs or drawings of public notices and signs. These notices and signs contain short sentences or phrases giving simple information, instructions or warnings. Next to each drawing or photograph are four sentences giving the meaning of the notice. Only one of the meanings is correct. You must choose the correct meaning.

When you first attempt this question, read every word of the text in the notice very carefully indeed. Try to guess what it means before you look at the four sentences next to it. When you have done this, read the four sentences. Then choose the sentence which you think agrees with your understanding of the notice.

> PT1.1, 2.7, 3.5, 6.2, PT2.1

‖ QUESTION 2 ‖

This question takes the form of a fairly short text which contains blanks. The text itself often tells a story or describes some events. Underneath the text a list of words is given to help you to complete the blanks. Four words are given for each blank, and you must choose the correct (or best) word for the blank.

When you begin this question, read all the text first before you look at the list of words below it. Try to understand what the passage is all about. When you have read the complete text, go back to the beginning and read the first sentence(s) carefully. Do not stop when you come to the first blank. Continue until the end of that particular sentence. Then look at the first four words given below the passage and choose the word which best completes that part of the sentence.

> PT1.2, 6.3, 6.6, PT2.2

‖ QUESTION 3 ‖

This question tests reading comprehension in a different way. Its aim is to test your understanding of certain facts and details in a text. Sometimes there are pictures with the text, and these pictures may also be used for the questions. Almost all the information in the text itself is important: hardly any additional and unnecessary information is given.

You should match the sentences following the text with the appropriate information in the text. You show your ability to do this by putting a tick in the correct box in a small table.

When you attempt this question, first look at all the information in the text. Don't worry about reading every word carefully. Read through the text as quickly as you can. Next read the sentences which follow the text. This time, however, read the sentences very carefully indeed. Look back at the text and try to match the information in each sentence with that given in the text. Check carefully after you have done each part of this question.

> PT1.3, 9.2, 10.6, 10.7, PT2.3

112

‖ QUESTION 4 ‖

This question often contains advertisements and various kinds of short descriptions. There are usually ten sentences based on the text. You must say whether each sentence is *True* or *False* (or answer *Yes* or *No*, etc) from the information contained in the text.

When you start to do this question, look at the text but don't try to read it. Look quickly at all the text and then read the first sentence carefully. Try to find the part of the text to which the sentence refers. If you think the sentence is correct, put a cross in the appropriate box. Check your answer again with the text and then do the second sentence in the same way.

PT1.4, 7.3, 14.1, 14.6, 14.7, PT2.4

‖ QUESTION 5 ‖

This question tests your ability to understand the general meaning of a passage and the writer's attitude to the subject. You must also be able to recognise the source from which the text was taken (eg a letter, a story, an advertisement). The reading comprehension passage is followed by various types of questions: eg multiple-choice, sentence completion, writing (short) answers to questions, and matching items.

Begin by reading quickly through the passage so that you can obtain an idea of the general meaning. After reading through the passage in this way, read through it again much more slowly and carefully. After this, read the first question and think about it carefully. Check your answer to the question with the appropriate part of the text itself (unless you have been asked to identify the source of the text, etc).

PT1.5, 9.4, 13.4, 15.4, 16.6, 16.8, PT25.

WRITING

‖ QUESTION 6 ‖

In this question you are given a sentence as a model and you must then write another sentence. The beginning of the new sentence is given, and you are asked to finish the sentence so that it has the same meaning as the model sentence.

When you do this part of the test, make sure that your new sentence really has a similar meaning to the original sentence. Make sure also that there are no mistakes of grammar. Sometimes you may produce the correct structure but you may make careless errors. Occasionally some students even fail to copy out phrases correctly from the model sentence.

PT1.6, 4.6, 4.7, 11.4, 14.5, 16.4, PT2.6

‖ QUESTION 7 ‖

In this question you are usually instructed to fill in a form or make notes. Sometimes you may be asked to leave a short message for someone. Although you will be expected to write about 75 words, it is not necessary for you to count the number of words.

If you have to fill in a form (usually with information about yourself), make sure you know the meaning of each of the following words and phrases: *surname, forenames, full name, initials, address, date of birth, age, nationality, occupation, qualifications, experience, hobbies/pastimes/sports, further information, accommodation, signature, date.*

If you make notes or write a message, remember that you can usually use short forms (eg *it's* = *it is; won't* = *will not*) and write in a style similar to spoken language (eg *Thanks* instead of *Thank you*).

PT1.7, 1.4, 7.7, 8.4, 8.7, 16.7, PT2.7

‖ QUESTION 8 ‖

Writing simple letters in English, giving accounts of events and describing plans are very important skills to practise. Don't write too much for this question and leave enough time to check your work very carefully indeed. About 100 words are required.

Write carefully and try to avoid making mistakes of grammar. If you are not sure about a certain grammatical point, avoid it. Use only those forms of language with which you are very familiar. Don't try to write long sentences and never use unfamiliar words in order to score high marks. Always write simply and clearly.

Even when you are asked to write a letter, you will not usually be asked to write your address. However, write the date and then begin your letter by writing either *Dear Mr/Mrs/Miss* + surname or *Dear* + forename. End your letter by writing either *Yours sincerely/Yours truly/Yours/With best wishes* + your own name (forename or full name).

> PT1.8, 9.3, 10.4, 12.5, 12.7, 12.8, 13.7, 16.9, PT2.8

LISTENING

In order to prepare thoroughly for this part of the test, you should listen as much as possible to people speaking English and to English programmes on the radio. In addition to understanding the words, try to understand the tone of each person's voice. Is the person who is speaking happy or sad? Is the person being funny or serious? All these clues will help you to understand what is being said.

‖ QUESTION 9 ‖

You will hear about seven statements or very short conversations on tape. Your ability to understand them is tested by means of simple drawings and photographs. Four of these pictures accompany each statement or conversation on the tape. You must choose the most appropriate picture for what you hear.

When you do this test, listen very carefully to the statement or conversation on the tape. Look at the four pictures in this part of the test while you are actually listening. Then choose the picture which you think most closely agrees with what you have heard. You will then hear the recording once again. This time check the picture as you listen.

> PT1.9, 2.5, 3.1, 3.7, PT2.9

‖ QUESTION 10 ‖

This question consists of a recording which contains information from travel and weather reports, events in the news, announcements, etc. Often it takes the form of a radio broadcast. As in the previous question, the recording is repeated so that you have a chance to check your answers and complete any questions which you may have missed.

The written questions about the talk are usually very short and do not require much reading. Usually they are multiple-choice questions, and you are required to put a tick in the correct box from a choice of four boxes.

> PT1.10, 7.8, 14.4, PT2.10

‖ QUESTION 11 ‖

This question may also take the form of a radio talk or report. Often it contains a report of things which have happened (eg a holiday or an excursion which someone has been on). Thus, it sometimes combines narrative with a piece of news or a report (including suggestions and advice). Once again, the talk is played twice.

Although some of the questions about the talk may require you to put ticks in boxes, other questions will require you to give short written answers, fill in blanks and take down numbers, etc. Always do as much as you can (ie by completing the written notes in the test book, etc) while you listen to the first playing of the talk. Then go over your answers during the second playing of the talk. Carefully check each answer and complete it where necessary.

If you cannot give an answer during either the first playing or the second playing of the talk, don't spend time thinking about the answer. Forget about it and pay attention to the remainder of the talk. If you spend too long thinking about an answer, you will miss the information given later in the talk.

> PT1.11, 5.5, 6.4, 8.5, 11.6, PT2.11

‖ QUESTION 12 ‖

The last question in the listening section takes the form of a recording of a discussion between two or three people. The people taking part in the discussion will usually talk about a subject in which they are both interested: eg buying a house, living in a certain area, going to a certain place for a holiday, remembering something interesting, amusing or unusual which happened to both of them, etc. Again, the discussion is played twice.

The written questions on the discussion usually take the form of *Yes/No* or *True/False* questions. Several statements (usually five) are given and you have to say whether you agree with them or not (ie whether you think they are true or false). The questions will test your ability to recognise whether the speakers agree or disagree with each other, whether they like or dislike something, whether they are apologising or complaining, etc.

PT1.12, 4.3, 12.2, 13.3, 15.6, 15.7, 16.3, PT2.12

SPEAKING

The oral part of the test involves both listening and speaking, and it lasts about 10 minutes. You may be tested either individually or in pairs. The more you practise speaking before the test, the easier you will find this part of the test. Speaking English should not be something which you do only a few weeks before the test. Try to speak as much English as you can all the time you are learning English. Speak in English to your teacher and to any English-speaking person you meet. Don't worry too much about making mistakes: above all, don't worry about losing face and feeling foolish. Speaking a foreign language is often the hardest skill to master, and so you must always try to practise as much as possible. Try to make your conversations form part of a real situation or activity.

Note that it is possible to take this part of the test either individually (ie one candidate with an examincr) or in pairs (ie two candidates with an examiner).

‖ SECTION I ‖

In this section, the examiner will give you a chance to settle down and overcome your nervousness. Don't worry too much if you cannot understand something the examiner says. This sometimes happens in conversations in real life between native-speakers. Say something like the following:

I'm sorry. I didn't understand what you said.
or *Sorry. I didn't catch that.*
or *Would you mind repeating that, please?*

The examiner will want to know all about you: your home, your family, your studies, your hobbies, etc. Try to talk as much as possible and avoid giving one-word answers. If you don't know much about the subject, change the conversation a little if you can. Try to talk naturally and avoid reciting something which you have carefully learnt.

During the conversation in this part, you will probably be asked to spell a word (eg your name, the name of the street where you live, etc) or read out a number (eg your candidate's number, your telephone number, your postal code, etc.)

If you take this section in pairs, you will have to ask the other candidate everyday questions about where he or she lives, why he or she is learning English. etc.

PT1.I, 1.6, PT2.I

‖ SECTION II ‖

In this section you may be asked to talk about any of the following:

what you need or want (ie needs);
how much something costs (ie prices);
how to get to a certain place (ie directions).

You may also have to make requests, offers of help and suggestions. Even if you don't do this, you will probably have to reply to requests, offers and suggestions from the examiner or from the other person attending the interview with you.

Unlike in Section I, you will be required to take part in a simple role-play. The examiner will describe a particular situation to you at the beginning of this part of the speaking test. As he speaks, he will give you a picture connected with the situation he is describing. For example, the examiner may tell you that you are in a large department store and want to buy a travel iron. He will give you a drawing or photograph of the type of iron you want to buy. Then he will play the part of a shop assistant, and you must talk to him about the iron which you want to buy.

If you take this section in pairs, you will be required to have a short conversation. For example, you may have some information about a good film and telephone the other student to ask him or her to go to see the film. Both of you would like to see the film very much but you are very busy. You both must try to find a day and a time when you can go together.

PT1.II, 5.4, 5.7, 6.5, 7.2
13.5, 14.2, 15.1, 16.2, PT2.II

‖ SECTION III ‖

You will have a short time to look at a colour photograph, a drawing or the cover of a brochure. You will later be asked to talk about it and to describe the people, objects and places in the picture. You must say what the people are doing and where the various objects are. Although the examiner will not ask questions for you to answer about the picture, he may say something to you in order to help you to talk.

You should start to talk about the picture by describing the most important part of it. This will usually be a person, an animal or an object in the middle of the picture, especially in the foreground of the picture (ie the part towards the front of the scene). Don't describe any details at first unless something is extremely important. After you have talked about what is happening, etc, you can begin to describe the detail (generally moving from the front of the scene to the background).

Don't be afraid to use your imagination. You can see what is happening in the picture, but what do you think has just happened? What is going to happen? Why?

If you are taking the speaking test in pairs, you and your partner will have to talk together about two similar pictures. You will try to find out in what ways the pictures are similar and in what ways they are different.

PT1.III, 9.5, 9.6, 13.8, PT2.III

‖ SECTION IV ‖

In this section you will be asked to talk mostly about what you like and dislike. This will be a general conversation about your experience, interests, and habits.

The conversation will use the picture in Section III as a starting point. If you do not know much about the activity in the picture (or if you are not very interested in it), the examiner will probably want you to talk about an activity, etc which you do like. For example, if you are shown a picture of someone in a rowing boat in Section III, the examiner may ask you if you have been rowing or if you like rowing – or indeed if you like sailing, etc. If you tell the examiner that you dislike boating (and say why) or if you tell the examiner that you have never been in a boat, the examiner will then ask you about something else.

Practise talking about the things you like and the things you dislike. Always remember to give a reason for your likes or dislikes.

If you are taking the speaking test in pairs, you and your partner will have to find out and discuss each other's interests, likes and dislikes.

PT1.IV, 13.2, 13.8, 13.9, PT2.IV

PICTURES AND ACTIVITIES FOR PAIRWORK

(Note that the page references refer to the appropriate pages where the activities appear in the book.)

‖ PRACTICE TEST 1: SECTION II
(SPEAKING: A) ‖
Page 24

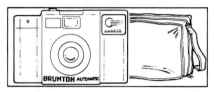

‖ PRACTICE TEST 1: SECTION II
(SPEAKING: B) ‖
Page 26

‖ PRACTICE TEST 1: SECTION III
(SPEAKING: A) ‖
Page 25

See the middle section of this book (ie the colour photographs).

‖ PRACTICE TEST 1: SECTION III
(SPEAKING: B) ‖
Page 27

See the middle section of this book (ie the colour photographs).

‖ Unit 5: Section 2 ‖
Page 46

Mon	Tues	Wed	Thurs	Fri	Sat
8.30–9.00 Mrs Chan	8.30–9.00 Mr Gobin	8.30–9.00	8.30–9.00 Mrs Omar	8.30–9.00 Miss Sibisi	8.30–9.00 Mr Ari
9.00–9.30 Miss Gambo	9.00–9.30 Mr Rosado	9.00–9.30 Mr Au	9.00–9.30 Mr Khandaker	9.00–9.30	9.00–9.30 Mr Smith
9.30–10.00 Mr Hall	9.30–10.00	9.30–10.00 Miss Jalil	9.30–10.00 Miss Kurma	9.30–10.00 Mrs Matas	9.30–10.00 Mr Brella
10.00–10.30	10.00–10.30 Mr Viadis	10.00–10.30 Mr Hill	10.00–10.30 Mrs Fung	10.00–10.30 Mr Akamazu	10.00–10.30
10.45–11.15 Mr Li	10.45–11.15 Mrs Fallah	10.45–11.15 Mr Habbu	10.45–11.15	10.45–11.15 Mr Tandon	10.45–11.15 Mrs Sharkas
11.15–11.45 Mr Ugar	11.15–11.45	11.15–11.45 Mrs Jones	11.15–11.45	11.15–11.45	11.15–11.45
11.45–12.45 Mrs Oner	11.45–12.45 Miss Azimi	11.45–12.45 Mr Marak	11.45–12.45 Mr Roy	11.45–12.45	11.45–12.45 Mr Akbari

‖ UNIT 5: SECTION 4 ‖
Page 47

Work in pairs.

STUDENT A:

Last week you bought the small exercise machine in the picture above. However, the handle has just come off the spring and you cannot use it. Several of your friends have also bought one but nothing has gone wrong with theirs. You take it back to the shop and ask for a new machine. If they haven't got any left, you want your money back.

‖ UNIT 5: SECTION 7 ‖
Page 48

STUDENT A:

Look at the notice below about a new health and fitness club. They are obviously looking for new members but you hear that it is quite expensive to join the club. Telephone Student B, tell him/her about the notice and ask him/her to go with you. (You want to look at the club but you aren't too keen on swimming.)

Bramhope Health and Fitness Club	
This week only! Visit our superb gymnasium and try out our new exercise machines **FREE OF CHARGE!** Monday, March 18 – Friday, March 22 18.30 – 22.00	And use our swimming pool for only £1.00!

‖ UNIT 6: SECTION 1 ‖
Page 49

STUDENT B:

Look at MAP B and then complete as much as possible of the table on page 49.
Next exchange information orally with your partner. In this way, you should both help each other to complete the table *without looking at each other's map*.

Today's weather
MAP B (ONLY *Student B should look at this map*)

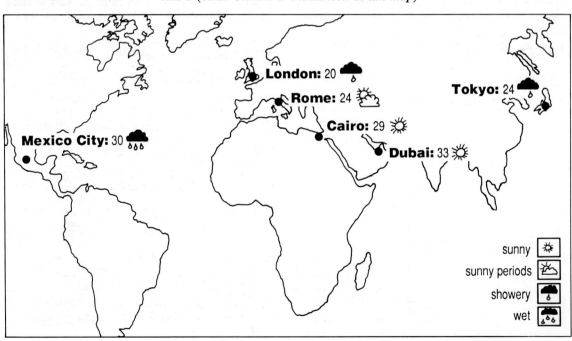

|| UNIT 6 SECTION 5 ||
Page 52

STUDENT B:

Look at the table below and answer Student A's questions. Advise A about visiting the places in the table. After finishing this, stop looking at the table and turn back to page 52.

STUDENT A:

Now look at the table below and answer Student B's questions.

Notes: (1) = maximum temperature (Centigrade)
(2) = minimum temperature (Centigrade)
− = a month with less than 1/12 of the annual rainfall
+ = a month with more than 1/12 of the annual rainfall
★ = the month(s) with the highest rainfall of the year

		Jan	Feb	Mar	Apr	May	Jun	Jul	Aug	Sep	Oct	Nov	Dec
Delhi	(1)	21	24	31	36	41	39	36	34	34	34	29	23
	(2)	7	9	14	20	26	28	27	26	24	18	11	8
		−	−	−	−	−	+	★	★	+	−	−	−
Hong Kong	(1)	18	17	19	24	28	29	31	31	29	27	23	20
	(2)	13	13	16	19	23	26	26	26	25	23	18	15
		−	−	−	−	+	★	★	★	+	−	−	−
Melbourne	(1)	26	26	24	20	17	14	13	15	17	19	22	24
	(2)	14	14	13	11	8	7	6	6	8	9	11	12
		−	−	+	+	−	−	−	−	+	★	+	+
Rio de Janeiro	(1)	29	29	28	27	25	24	24	24	24	25	26	28
	(2)	23	23	22	21	19	18	17	18	18	19	20	22
		+	+	+	+	−	−	−	−	−	−	+	★

|| UNIT 7: SECTION 5 ||
Page 55

STUDENT B:

Look at the incomplete plan below. It shows the places to which trains travel from Tokyo. It also shows the times taken to travel to these places. Ask Student A questions and also answer his/her questions so that you can complete your plans.

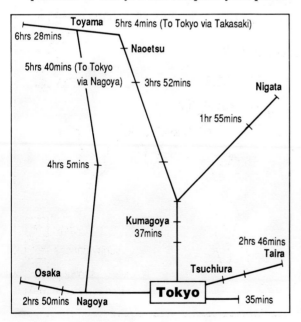

|| UNIT 8: SECTION 6 ||
Page 60

STUDENT A:

You have the following information about English language courses in Britain. A few people (ie other members of your group) phone you and ask you about certain English courses. Answer their questions and give as much advice as you can.

Purley Language Centre
25 Westbourne Road, Sussex
English for Foreign Students
Full-time courses only
All ages
All levels
Residential accommodation
Fees: £180 per week (tuition and accommodation)

South London Tutorial College
Brighton Road, Croydon
Students prepared both individually and in small groups for leading UK examinations. All subjects taught but foreign students especially welcome.
Good intensive English courses. Part-time and full-time.
Help found with accommodation if requested
Fees: £5 per hour

Kensington School of English
Brompton Road, Kensington, London
English courses for children
(aged 6 to 11)
Language activities, games, videos.
This is the perfect place for a short holiday course for children.

Visits to museums and other places of interest.
Fees: £140 per week: 10% reduction for parties of 6 or more.

Multi-Lingual House
Stoke Square, Durham
Learn English, French, German, Spanish, Italian, Arabic and Chinese in a large country house.
Short, high-quality intensive courses.
Individual tuition and tuition in small groups.
Language lab, computers and video facilities.
Superb residential accommodation.
Total fees: £760 per week.

Lake District English Centre
Bowness Centre, Grasmere
Holiday English Courses
Go climbing, walking, cycling, canoeing and sailing AND improve your English at the same time!
English classes in the mornings and activities in the afternoons and at weekends.
Comfortable accommodation in old cottages surrounded by beautiful mountains and lakes.
Evening social activities.
Fees: £340 per week (includes tuition, accommodation, food, and hire of all equipment)
(Open: 1 May – 30 September)

English Language Institute
11–15 Royal Mile, Edinburgh
English for Special Purposes
Business English our speciality
Long and short courses throughout the year apart from January
RSA Diploma Courses
Special 10-week intensive courses in teaching English as a foreign language
Fees: £180–£220 a week.
Accommodation (about £90 a week with families)

‖ UNIT 9: SECTION 5 ‖
Page 64

Only Student A should look at this photograph.

STUDENT A:
Talk about the photograph to Student B and answer any questions which Student B asks.
Remember to describe
the persons' faces
their clothes and general appearance
what they are doing
what they may be thinking
any other important details in the picture

After you have finished talking about it, listen to Student B describe the photograph which he/she is looking at. Ask any questions you want about it. Try to form as clear a picture as you can of B's photograph. Finally, look at B's photograph. In what way is it different from what you expected? How could B have described it more accurately?

‖ UNIT 9: SECTION 6 ‖
Page 65

Only Student B should look at this photograph.

STUDENT B:

Talk about the photograph to Student A.

Then listen to Student A talk about his/her photograph and try to find out how the two photographs are similar and how they are different. Later, show Student A your photograph and discuss the two photographs.

‖ UNIT 12: SECTION 3 ‖
Page 74

STUDENT B:

Copy out the table below into your exercise book.

1 Pretend to interview Student A for the first job. Ask questions to find out Student A's ability to do a job as a **technician** and fill in the first line of the table.

2 After asking questions, you must then let Student A interview you. Student A will ask you questions about your ability to do a job as a **nurse**. You must use the information in the table to answer the questions.

3 Now change parts once again and ask Student A questions about his/her ability to do a job as a **reporter**. Work through the table in this way.

Student B's table

Job	Reason for applying	Ability to do the job	Attitudes	When able to start
Technician				
Nurse	Interested	Helpful to all	Keen	6 months
Reporter				
Clerk	Wants desk job near home	Types fast	Not too keen	Not known
Soldier				
Teacher	Likes children	Good at maths	Attracted by long holidays	September

‖ UNIT 13: SECTION 5 ‖
Page 79

STUDENT B:

You are a librarian. Look at the titles of some books in the library. Listen to Student A and suggest some books which will be suitable for him/her.

The Book of the Countryside   Lola Blanco
The World's Coins: An Illustrated Guide   Philip Burns
Learn to Swim   Rosanna de Maria
Radio Times   Martin Lee
Gardening Throughout the Year   Alex Izak
Japanese Flower Arrangement   Hiroko Asano
The World's Best Photographs of 1989   Sheila Mantillet
Making Money at Home   Paul Dunning

Water Sports   Shigeru Ichi
Nuttons Guide to Arts and Crafts   Svetlana Tsintsdaze
Taking Photos for Pleasure and Profit   Marcia Sillito
Your Radio: A Guide to Wavelengths and Tuning   Tsao Ming Liang
Model Aeroplanes   Ken Pilgram
Guide to New and Used Cameras   Wipa Suvarnakich

‖ UNIT 13: SECTION 6 ‖
Page 79

STUDENT A:

Look at the information which follows. Then answer all Student B's questions about holidays for people who are keen on driving. You have heard excellent reports about the motor racing holidays at the BSO Racing School. Talk about all three holidays.

BSO Racing School Elm Road, Rigton. Tel. Rigton 756623 Weekend introductory course to motor racing. All year. Including 5 hours expert instruction at a famous race track. Age 18+, £180 including meals and accommodation. Individuals, families and groups of up to 20 in single, double and shared rooms.	**Blue Mountain Hotel** Kirkby, Humberside Tel: 0482-877610 Driving weekends. Rally driving, motor racing and advanced driving. Also fascinating tours of the beautiful Humberside country. From £78 bed and breakfast for 2 nights. Lunch and dinner extra. No groups of over 10. Comfortable single and double rooms available in the hotel.	**Motor Fun Ltd** 502 Pannal Road, Ripon Tel. 0765-3341 Driving holidays: 1 day to 7 nights. Adventure and fun, off-road adventure parks, different kinds of cars. Full instruction from beginners to advanced drivers. Also motor racing instruction May to September (small extra charge). From £25 per night not including meals. Rooms with families.

▌ UNIT 14: SECTION 2 ▐
Page 83

STUDENT A:
> You work in the box office of a theatre. Look at the theatre seating plan below and answer Student B's questions, helping him/her to book as good seats as possible.

Grand Theatre: Seating plan (Stalls)
(Only Student A should look at this plan.)

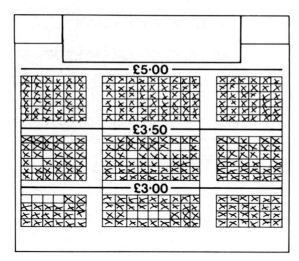

After finishing this activity, turn back to page 83.

STUDENT B:
> Pretend to work in the booking office and book seats for Student A.

Grand Theatre: Seating plan (Circle)
(Only Student B should look at this plan.)

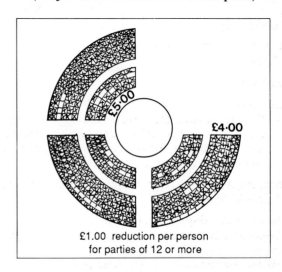

£1.00 reduction per person
for parties of 12 or more

▌ UNIT 15: SECTION 1 ▐
Page 87

Only Student A should look at this map.

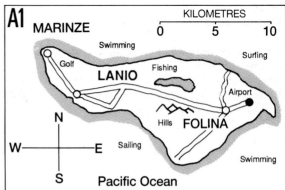

‖ UNIT 15: SECTION 1 ‖
Page 87

Only Student B should look at this map.

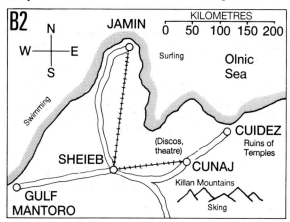

‖ UNIT 16: SECTION 2 ‖
Page 91

Activity 1

STUDENT B:

You are a waiter. Help Student A to choose suitable dishes. Look at the detailed information about the various dishes before you try to answer Student A's questions and give advice.

Student B should look at this first and later Student A should look at it.

Soup of the day: Tomato soup
Cocktail à la maison: Cherries, pieces of pineapple, apples, pears and oranges
Home-made pate: Chicken liver pate
Parma ham and melon: Very thin pieces of raw ham with a slice of melon
Chef's speciality: Beef steak with a pepper sauce, boiled potatoes and peas
Swiss fondue: Melted cheese with small pieces of bread
Risotto Milanese: Rice, salami slices, tomato sauce
Lamb à la maison: Leg of lamb, roast potatoes and mint sauce
Shepherd's pie: Minced beef and mashed potatoes
Lobster salad: Half a lobster on lettuce and cold potatoes with mayonnaise

Grilled Dover sole: Fresh fish grilled (not fried) topped with butter and lemon and served with chips
Sherry trifle: Fruit, custard and jelly in layers (with some sherry added)
Cumbrian pudding: Hot lemon sponge pudding and custard
Black Forest gateaux: Chocolate and cherry cake
Cheese: Gruyere (French), Danish Blue, Stilton (English) or Wensleydale (English)

Activity 2

STUDENT A:

You are now a waiter. Help Student B to choose suitable dishes. Look at the detailed information about the various dishes before you try to answer Student B's questions and give advice.

‖ PRACTICE TEST 2: SECTION II ‖
Page 111

STUDENT A:

Telephone Student B and tell him/her about this exhibition. Ask him/her to go with you and arrange a convenient time.

LEETRONEX UNIVERSITY

DEPARTMENT OF ENGINEERING

EXHIBITION

Come and see all the latest equipment and interesting demonstrations

16 June – 19 June

Monday – Wednesday 10 am – 7 pm
Thursday 10 am – 4 pm

‖ PRACTICE TEST 2: SECTION III ‖
Page 111

See the middle section of this book (ie the colour photographs).

We are grateful to the following, for permission to
reproduce copyright photographic material in this book:

Ace Photo Agency for page ii (bottom), Barnaby's Picture
Library/Brian G. Turner for page 81 (bottom), Bolton
Stirland International for page 118, Camera Press for
page 65 (bottom), J. Allan Cash for pages 65 (top) and
81 (top), Longman/John Birdsall for page 120 (bottom),
Longman Photographic Unit for page 120 (top),
Longman/St. John Pope for pages iii and iv, Picturepoint
for page ii (top), Sporting Pictures (UK) Ltd for page i.

We are grateful to the following, for permission to
reproduce copyright material:

T.G. Holdcroft Motors Ltd for page 101, London
Regional Transport for use of the Corporation's
Underground Map on page 54, Sunwin Motors of
Bradford for page 101, USA Today for page 14, Vincents
Cars Reading for page 100.

Illustrated by Chris Pavely